W9-DCX-101

ANT HOMES

Under THE GROUND

Teacher's Guide
Preschool–1

Skills
Observing, Comparing, Communicating, Role Playing, Cooperative Work, Counting, Problem Solving, Spatial Reasoning, Computation, Gathering Data

Concepts
Ant Body Structure, Feeding, Life Cycle, Defense, Cooperation, Communication, Social Behavior, Community Jobs, Number Sense, Pattern Recognition

Themes
Systems and Interactions, Patterns of Change,
Models and Simulations, Scale, Structure, Diversity and Unity
(See page 108 for more information about themes.)

Mathematics Strands
Number, Logic and Language, Pattern, Statistics

Nature of Science and Mathematics
Cooperative Efforts, Real-Life Applications, Interdisciplinary

by
Jean C. Echols
Kimi Hosoume
Jaine Kopp

LHS GEMS

GEMS
Great Explorations in Math and Science
Lawrence Hall of Science
University of California at Berkeley

Lawrence Hall of Science
　　Chairman: Glenn T. Seaborg
　　Director: Ian Carmichael

Initial support for the origination and publication of the GEMS series was provided by the A.W. Mellon Foundation and the Carnegie Corporation of New York. GEMS has received support from the McDonnell-Douglas Foundation and the McDonnell-Douglas Employees Community Fund, the Hewlett Packard Company Foundation, and the people at Chevron USA. GEMS gratefully acknowledges the contribution of word processing equipment from Apple Computer, Inc. This support does not imply responsibility for statements or views expressed in publications of the GEMS program.

Under a grant from the National Science Foundation, GEMS Leader's Workshops have been held across the country. For further information on GEMS leadership opportunities, or to receive a publication brochure and the GEMS Network News, please contact GEMS at the address and phone number provided.

Development of this guide was sponsored in part by the Department of Education Fund for the Improvement of Post-Secondary Education (FIPSE) and a grant from the National Science Foundation.

COMMENTS WELCOME

Great Explorations in Math and Science (GEMS) is an ongoing curriculum development project. GEMS guides are revised periodically, to incorporate teacher comments and new approaches. We welcome your criticisms, suggestions, helpful hints, and any anecdotes about your experience presenting GEMS activities. Your suggestions will be reviewed each time a GEMS guide is revised. Please send your comments to:

　　University of California, Berkeley
　　GEMS Revisions
　　Lawrence Hall of Science #5200
　　Berkeley, CA 94720-5200

Our phone number is (510) 642-7771.
Our fax number is (510) 643-0309.

GEMS STAFF

Principal Investigator
　Glenn T. Seaborg
Director
　Jacqueline Barber
Associate Directors
　Kimi Hosoume, Lincoln Bergman
Science Curriculum Specialist
　Cary Sneider
Mathematics Curriculum Specialist
　Jaine Kopp
GEMS Sites and Centers Coordinator
　Carolyn Willard
GEMS Workshop Coordinator
　Laura Tucker
GEMS Workshop Administrator
　Terry Cort
Staff Development Specialists
　Lynn Barakos, Katharine Barrett, Kevin
　Beals, Ellen Blinderman, Beatrice Boffen,
　Gigi Dornfest, John Erickson,
　Stan Fukunaga, Philip Gonsalves,
　Cathy Larripa, Laura Lowell,
　Linda Lipner, Debra Sutter
Administrative Coordinator
　Cynthia Eaton
Distribution Coordinator
　Karen Milligan
Distribution Representative
　Felicia Roston
Shipping Assistants
　Ben Arreguy, George Kasarjian
Trial Testing Coordinator
　Stephanie Van Meter
Senior Editor
　Carl Babcock
Editor
　Florence Stone
Public Information Representative
　Gerri Ginsburg
Principal Publications Coordinator
　Kay Fairwell
Art Director
　Lisa Haderlie Baker
Designers
　Carol Bevilacqua, Rose Craig, Lisa Klofkorn
Staff Assistants
　Kasia Bukowinski, Larry Gates,
　Nick Huynh, Steve Lim, Nancy Lin,
　Michelle Mahogany, Karla Penuelas,
　Alisa Sramala

©1996 by The Regents of the University of California. All rights reserved.
Printed in the United States of America. International Standard Book Number (ISBN): 0-912511-99-0.

Great Explorations in Math and Science (GEMS) Program

The Lawrence Hall of Science (LHS) is a public science center on the University of California at Berkeley campus. LHS offers a full program of activities for the public, including workshops and classes, exhibits, films, lectures, and special events. LHS is also a center for teacher education and curriculum research and development.

Over the years, LHS staff developed a multitude of activities, assembly programs, classes, and interactive exhibits. These programs have proven to be successful at LHS and should be useful to schools, other science centers, museums, and community groups. A number of these guided-discovery activities are published under the Great Explorations in Math and Science (GEMS) title, after an extensive refinement process that includes classroom testing of trial versions, modifications to ensure the use of easy-to-obtain materials, and carefully written and edited step-by-step instructions and background information to allow presentation by teachers without special background in mathematics or science.

Contributing Authors

Jacqueline Barber
Katharine Barrett
Kevin Beals
Lincoln Bergman
Beverly Braxton
Kevin Cuff
Celia Cuomo
Linda De Lucchi
Gigi Dornfest
Jean Echols
John Erickson
Philip Gonsalves
Jan M. Goodman
Alan Gould
Catherine Halversen
Kimi Hosoume
Sue Jagoda
Jaine Kopp
Linda Lipner
Laura Lowell
Larry Malone
Cary I. Sneider
Craig Strang
Debra Sutter
Rebecca Tilley
Jennifer Meux White
Carolyn Willard

ACKNOWLEDGMENTS

Photographs: Richard Hoyt
Illustrations and Cover: Rose Craig

Thanks to all the enthusiastic people at the Lawrence Hall of Science, including **Katharine Barrett, Beatrice Boffen,** and **Bernadette Lauraya,** for their suggestions and other contributions during the development and writing of *Ant Homes Under the Ground.* Special thanks go to **Ellen Blinderman** for her many original ideas, inspiration, and encouragement.

Thanks to **Loy Volkman, Jan Washburn,** and **Judi Pascocello** of the University of California at Berkeley's Department of Entomology and Parasitology for their scientific review of this guide.

Thanks to teachers **Leslie Cooper, Dorothy Harris, Linda Luzar,** and **Judy Ogata** of Redwood Heights Elementary School in Oakland, California, and **Karen Fong** and **Margaret Brockway** of Sequoia Nursery School in Oakland, California, for the generous gift of their time in allowing us to photograph this guide's activities in their classrooms. And, of course, thanks to all the children who enliven the photographs in this guide.

REVIEWERS

We would like to thank the following educators who reviewed, tested, or coordinated the reviewing of this series of GEMS/PEACHES materials in manuscript and draft form. Their critical comments and recommendations, based on presentation of these activities nationwide, contributed significantly to these GEMS publications. Their participation in the review process does not necessarily imply endorsement of the GEMS program or responsibility for statements or views expressed. Their role is an invaluable one, and their feedback is carefully recorded and integrated as appropriate into the publications.

ALASKA
Coordinator:
Cynthia Dolmas Curran

Creative Play Preschool, Wasilla
Ronda Ingham
Mary Percak-Dennett

Iditarod Elementary School, Wasilla
Beverly McPeek

Wasilla Middle School, Wasilla
Cynthia Dolmas Curran

ARKANSAS
Coordinator: **Lucy Bikulcs**

Goose Bay Elementary School, Palmer
Lucy Bikulcs
Lisa Gigo
Kathleen Godsoe
Deborah Waisanen

ARIZONA
Coordinator: **Mary Jo Eckhardt**

Julia Randall Elementary School, Payson
Mary Jo Eckhardt
Terri Legassie
Kay Wilson

Payson Head Start, Payson
Dani Rosenstell

CALIFORNIA
Coordinators: **Leslie Cooper, Karen Fong, Kathy Moran, Floria Spencer, Rebecca Wheat, Dottie Wiggins**

4C's Children's Center, Oakland
Yolanda Coleman-Wilson

24 Hour Children Center, Oakland
Sheryl Lambert
Ella Tassin
Inez Watson

Afterschool Program, Piedmont
Willy Chen

Alameda Head Start, Alameda
Michelle Garabedian
Debbie Garcia
Stephanie Josey

Albany Children's Center, Albany
Celestine Whittaker

Bancroft School, Berkeley
Cecilia Saffarian

Bartell Childcare and Learning Center, Oakland
Beverly Barrow
Barbara Terrell

Beach Elementary School, Piedmont
Ann Blasius
Juanita Forester
Elodee Lessley
Jean Martin

Belle Vista Child Development Center, Oakland
Satinder Jit K. Rana

Berkeley-Albany YMCA, Berkeley
Trinidad Caselis

Berkeley Hills Nursery School, Berkeley
Elizabeth Fulton

Berkeley/Richmond Jewish Community, Berkeley
Terry Amgott-Kwan

Berkeley Unified School District, Berkeley
Rebecca Wheat

Berkwood-Hedge School, Berkeley
Elizabeth Wilson

Bernice & Joe Play School, Oakland
Bernice Huisman-Humbert

Bing School, Stanford
Kate Ashbey

Brookfield Elementary School, Oakland
Kathy Hagerty
Linda Rogers

Brookfield Head Start, Oakland
Suzie Ashley

Butte Kiddie Corral, Shingletown
Cindy Stinar Black

Cedar Creek Montessori, Berkeley
Idalina Cruz
Jeanne Devin
Len Paterson

Centro Vida, Berkeley
Rosalia Wilkins

Chinese Community United Methodist Church, Oakland
Stella Ko Kwok

Clayton Valley Parent Preschool, Concord
Lee Ann Sanders
Patsy Sherman

Compañeros del Barrio State Preschool, San Francisco
Anastasia Decaristos
Laura Todd

Contra Costa College, San Pablo
Sylvia Alvarez-Mazzi

Creative Learning Center, Danville
Brooke H. B. D'Arezzo

Creative Play Center, Pleasant Hill
Debbie Coyle
Sharon Keane

Dena's Day Care, Oakland
Kawsar Elshinawy

Dover Preschool, Richmond
Alice J. Romero

Duck's Nest Preschool, Berkeley
Pierrette Allison
Patricia Foster
Mara Ellen Guckian
Ruth Major

East Bay Community Children's Center, Oakland
Charlotte Johnson
Oletha R. Wade

Ecole Bilingue, Berkeley
Nichelle R. Kitt
Richard Mermis
Martha Ann Reed

Emerson Child Development Center, Oakland
Ron Benbow
Faye McCurtis
Vicky Wills

Emerson Elementary School, Oakland
Pamela Curtis-Horton

Emeryville Child Development Center, Emeryville
Ellastine Blalock
Jonetta Bradford
Ortencia A. Hoopii

Enrichment Plus Albert Chabot School, Oakland
Lisa Dobbs

Family Day Care, Oakland
Cheryl Birden
Penelope Brody
Eufemia Buena Byrd
Mary Waddington

Family Day Care, Orinda
Lucy Inouye

Gan Hillel Nursery School, Richmond
Denise Moyes-Schnur

Gan Shalom Preschool, Berkeley
Iris Greenbaum

Garner Toddler Center, Alameda
Uma Srinath

Gay Austin, Albany
Sallie Hanna-Rhyne

Giggles Family Day Care, Oakland
Doris Wührmann

Greater Richmond Social Services Corp., Richmond
Lucy Coleman

Happy Lion School, Pinole
Sharon Espinoza
Marilyn Klemm

Hintil Kuu Ca Child Development Center, Oakland
Eunice C. Blago
Kathy Moran
Gina Silber
Agnes Tso
Ed Willie

Jack-in-the-Box Junction Preschool, Richmond
Virginia Guadarrama

Kinder Care, Oakland
Terry Saugstad

King Child Development Center, Berkeley
Joan Carr
Diane Chan
Frances Stephens
Eula Webster
Dottie Wiggins

King Preschool, Richmond
Charlie M. Allums

The Lake School, Oakland
Margaret Engel
Patricia House
Vickie Stoller

Learning Adventures Child Development, Redding
Dena Keown

Longfellow Child Development Center, Oakland
Katryna Ray

Los Medanos Community College, Pittsburg
Judy Henry
Filomena Macedo

Maraya's Developmental Center, Oakland
Maria A. Johnson-Price
Gayla Lucero

Mark Twain School Migrant Education, Modesto
Grace Avila

Mary Jane's Preschool, Pleasant Hill
Theresa Borges

Merritt College Children's Center, Oakland
Deborah Green
Virginia Shelton

Mickelson's Child Care, Ramona
Levata Mickelson

Mills College Children's Center, Oakland
Monica Grycz

Mission Head Start, San Francisco
Pilar Marroquin
Mirna Torres

The Model School Comprehensive, Berkeley
Jenny Schwartz-Groody

Montclair Community Play Center, Oakland
Elaine Guttmann
Nancy Kliszewski
Mary Loeser

Next Best Thing, Oakland
Denise Hingle
Franny Minervini-Zick

Oak Center Christian Academy, Oakland
Debra Booze

Oakland Parent Child Center, Oakland
Barbara Jean Jackson

Oakland Unified School District, Oakland
Floria Spencer

Orinda Preschool, Orinda
Tracy Johansing-Spittler

Oxford St. Learning Road, Berkeley
Vanna Maria Kalofonos

Peixoto Children's Center, Hayward
Alma Arias
Irma Guzman
Paula Lawrence
Tyra Toney

Piedmont Cooperative Playschool, Piedmont
Marcia Nybakken

Playmates Daycare, Berkeley
Mary T. McCormick

Rainbow School, Oakland
Mary McCon
Rita Neely

Redwood Heights Elementary
School, Oakland
Dorothy Harris
Leslie Cooper
Linda Luzar
Judy Ogata

San Antonio Head Start, Oakland
Cynthia Hammock
Ilda Terrazas

San Jose City College, San Jose
Mary Conroy

Sequoia Nursery School, Oakland
Margaret Brockway
Karen Fong
Lorraine Holmstedt

Sequoyah Community Preschool,
Oakland
Erin Smith
Kim Wilcox

Shakelford Head Start, Modesto
Teresa Avila

So Big Preschool, Antioch
Linda Kochly

St. Vincent's Day Home, Oakland
Pamela Meredith

Sunshine Preschool, Berkeley
Poppy Richie

U. C. Berkeley Child Care Services
Smyth Fernwald II, Berkeley
Diane Wallace
Caroline W. Yee

Walnut Ave. Community Preschool,
Walnut Creek
Evelyn DeLanis

Washington Child Development
Center, Berkeley
Reather Jones

Washington Kids Club, Berkeley
Adwoa A. Mante

Westview Children's Center, Pacifica
Adrienne J. Schneider

Woodroe Woods, Hayward
Wendy Justice

Woodstock Child Development
Center, Alameda
Mary Raabe
Denise M. Ratto

Woodstock School, Alameda
Amber D. Cupples

Yuk Yan Annex, Oakland
Eileen Lok

YWCA Oakland, Oakland
Iris Ezeb
Grace Perry

COLORADO
Coordinator: **Morrie Rupp**

Hotchkiss Elementary School,
Hotchkiss
Liz Cowman
Linda Hodges
Donna Hooker
Janet Oatman
Morrie Rupp
Fran Stein

DISTRICT OF
COLUMBIA
Coordinator: **Herbert Williams**

Barnard Elementary School,
Washington
Naya Bloom
Evelyn Lee
April Linder
Brenda Williams

MISSISSIPPI
Coordinator: **Josephine Gregory**

Little Village Child Development
Center, Jackson
Josephine Gregory
Patrick Gregory
Denise Harris
Barbara Johnson

NEW YORK
Coordinators: **Stephen Levey,**
Mary Jean Syrek

Aquarium for Wildlife Conservation,
Brooklyn
Meryl Kafka

Dr. Charles R. Drew Science Magnet,
Buffalo
Linda Edwards
Carol Podger
Diana Roberts
Willie Robinson
Mary Jean Syrek

PS 329—Surfside School, Brooklyn
Sharon Fine
Valerie LaManna
Stephen Levey
Barbara Nappo
Angela Natale
Arline Reisman

TEXAS
Coordinator: **Myra Luciano**

Armand Bayou Elementary School,
Houston
Myra Luciano
Judy Patrick
Jeanne Vining

John F. Ward Elementary School,
Houston
Brenad Greenshields
Luanne Lamar
Vicki Peterson
Jenny Scott

North Pointe Elementary School,
Houston
Phyllis Berman

WASHINGTON
Coordinator: **Peggy Willcuts**

Blue Ridge Mountain School,
Walla Walla
Elizabeth Arebalos
Sandi Burt
Gail Callahan
Leah Crudup
Peggy Willicuts

WEST VIRGINIA
Coordinator: **Beverly Keener**

Elk Elementary School, Charleston
Beverly Keener
Ruth Ann Reynolds
Cathy Securro
Deborah Wilson

CONTENTS

GEMS and PEACHES

GEMS is publishing a number of early childhood activity guides developed by the PEACHES project of the Lawrence Hall of Science. PEACHES is a curriculum development and training program for teachers and parents of children in preschool through first grade.

Like the GEMS guides already available for preschool and the early grades—such as *Hide A Butterfly*, *Animal Defenses*, and *Buzzing A Hive*—the PEACHES guides combine free exploration, drama, art, and literature with science and mathematics to give young children positive and effective learning experiences.

Introduction

An ant is one creature children are almost certain to see around them no matter where they live. Ants seem to be everywhere—in yards, on playgrounds, and often in homes and classrooms. Welcome or not, ants are interesting social insects. The variety of jobs they do, what they hide in their underground homes, and how and why they leave scent trails are fascinating topics for young children. This fascination in turn enlivens interest in insects and the natural world.

"The ant finds kingdoms in a foot of ground."
— Stephen Vincent Benet

Activities for a Wide Range of Abilities

The activities in *Ant Homes Under the Ground* are for children in preschool through first grade. Because of a wide range of abilities, some of the activities are more appropriate for younger children and others for older students. It is not necessary to do every activity with each age group.

For preschoolers, keep the activities short and introduce few concepts, facts, and new words in each session. Take advantage of every opportunity for role playing. The younger the children the more they enjoy pretending they are ants and crawling through tunnel-like structures. Older children can handle more discussion and more detailed observations.

The lesson descriptions include suggestions for modifying the activities to make them appropriate for the level of your students. For younger children, you may want to limit the section on the ant's life cycle. Children in preschool and kindergarten enjoy learning that ants lay eggs and seeing what baby ants look like. Children in first grade can go a step further and learn about the change that occurs in the ant during the pupal stage as it develops into an adult.

While the activities in *Ant Homes Under the Ground* are for children in preschool through first grade, they can be adapted for second and third graders. Involve older students in more language activities such as writing and illustrating a book on ants, or dramatizing an ant story for the whole class. Conducting more involved investigations with live ants outdoors is another appropriate activity for older students. Encourage them to find ways to discover whether ants have food preferences, are attracted to color, or are able to find a certain scent. They can keep journals of the ant observations they make and use the resource books on page 79 to research interesting information about ants. Also, older students can design a much more elaborate mural than younger children.

Some of the sessions in this book are short and can be combined with other sessions depending on your preferences and time constraints. The Going Further sections have suggestions for activities to extend the sessions.

Most of the activities in this book can be done in small groups or "learning centers." Arrange several days in advance for adults or older students to help with activities such as the walks to look for ants. The dramas and the role playing usually work well with the whole class.

Often we include questions to ask the children. Many of these questions are open-ended and encourage the children to come up with their own ideas. Their answers should give you insight into their thinking. All responses from the children should be recognized in a positive way. In this book, possible answers to the questions are included after the question in brackets [brackets]. These responses are some of the answers you might expect from your children. They are not meant to be used to correct the children or to give them the "right" answer. The bracketed answers are provided as a reference for you to clarify the information being addressed.

The Activities

As you go through these activities, you may want to develop a list of the important words the children will learn and use throughout the unit. You can make word cards or write them on the board or chart paper. Reviewing the words at the beginning of each activity should increase the activity's accessibility and its enjoyment for your students.

In **Activity 1**, the children have several opportunities to watch the fascinating behavior of live ants.

In Session 1: The Ant Hunt, the students share ant stories and go on an ant hunt outside to look for ants, anthills, and ant trails. They place a board or flat stone on dampened ground in an area where they find ants in hopes that ants will make their nest underneath.

In Session 2: The Ant Farm, they set up an Ant Farm and fill it with live ants. You and your students make a feeding and watering schedule so the children can take turns caring for the ants.

In **Activity 2**, the students concentrate on the ant's body structure and tunneling behavior. In Session 1: A Closer Look at Ants, the children count the ant's body parts and learn more about ants as they observe an Ant poster. They make their own paper ants, which become part of a classroom ant society.

In Session 2: Ant Tunnels, the youngsters become familiar with the tunneling activity of ants by observing live ants digging tunnels in the ant farm. The children observe sections 1 and 2 (Ant Tunnels) of the Ant Nest poster in which many ants work together digging tunnels and chambers. The boys and girls experience the darkness and confinement of a tunnel by pretending to be ants crawling through a tunnel-like structure. The class begins an ant nest mural and each child adds a paper chamber and two tunnels to the large sheet of paper.

The emphasis in **Activity 3** is on ant food. The children learn about the variety of foods ants eat, how ants move the food, and why they hide it inside their nest.

In Session 1: Scouts and Guards, the girls and boys pretend to be scout ants following a scent trail to a bag of crackers and carry the crackers back to an anthill to share. As "guard ants," several children stand at the entrance to the nest, protecting the nest from "enemy ants" by checking the scent of the "ants" that enter.

In Session 2: Dragging Food into the Nest, cooperative problem solving is encouraged as four children work together to move a large and awkward "caterpillar" across the room and into a "tunnel." The problem of how to fit a large object into a relatively small enclosed space challenges the children to decide whether to carry, push, or pull it through the tunnel. As with ants, teamwork is necessary to accomplish this task.

While looking at the Ant Nest poster in Session 3: More Ant Food, the children discover a caterpillar and a grasshopper in the ant nest. They see scout ants leaving the nest to look for food, guard ants protecting the nest, and housekeeper ants dragging dead ants away as they clean their home. The youngsters go outside to check the ant food and add an unusual morsel to their ant farm.

In **Activity 4**, the children are introduced to the life cycle of ants. They discover the queen ant in a chamber on the Ant Nest poster. They learn the queen ant lays all the eggs, and nurse ants take care of the eggs and baby ants. They also learn about other jobs that ants do as part of the ant community.

As the children decide what jobs they want their paper ants to do, they expand the Ant Nest mural by adding paper food, eggs, and baby ants. The children begin to realize that it takes many different workers doing many different jobs to keep an ant nest and society functioning.

In **Activity 5**, children work with an "anthill" game board to reinforce their knowledge of ants and to practice important mathematics skills. They are counting in context, which supports one-to-one correspondence as well as number/quantity relationships. The children do simple addition using their game boards and develop spatial orientation and visualization discrimination skills. Cooperative work skills are encouraged. The mathematics is in the context of real-world experiences so it has more meaning.

In Session 1, the children focus on the various jobs that ants do as they have fun filling the game board with plastic ants, food, and eggs. They independently place items on the game board and spontaneously share stories about their filled anthills. In Session 2, they work with a partner to place items on the game boards—this time it is a cooperative venture to prepare them for the last session of the activity. In Session 3, children play a specially designed cooperative logic game that allows partners to collaboratively "Fill the Hill" according to the directions on a set of four cards.

If you enjoy investigating ants with your students, you may wish to consider these other GEMS units for this age: Buzzing A Hive, Ladybugs, Hide A Butterfly, *and* Terrarium Habitats.

For additional cooperative activities, the GEMS guide Group Solutions *encourages cooperative learning.*

Included for your use are: Literature Connections to the various activities, Background Information about ants, Resources on where to find out more about ants and where to obtain the live ants, and Assessment Suggestions so you can gauge how well your students grasped the concepts in this unit. In the back of the guide, for your copying ease, are extra perforated sheets of the game cards, game board, and large ant. Also, in the back of the guide are the large fold-out, perforated pages of the Ant Nest poster.

Finally, creative play and cooperative skills are important parts of this unit. As the girls and boys play freely within the activities, they often remember and act out real animal behavior using concepts presented in this unit. As the children share their experiences of many mathematical concepts and skills, their observations of ants, and create their own ant stories, their language and mathematical skills develop in fun and spontaneous ways.

Activity 1: Ants, Ants, Ants

Overview

Observing ants in their natural setting is one of the most valuable ways to learn about ants, and one that is fun and exciting for children. In this activity, the children have several opportunities to watch the fascinating behavior of live ants.

In Session 1: The Ant Hunt, the students share ant stories and go on an ant hunt to look for ants, anthills, and ant trails. They place a board or flat stone on dampened ground in an area where they find ants in hope the ants will make a nest underneath.

In Session 2: The Ant Farm, the children set up an Ant Farm and fill it with live ants. You and your students make a feeding and watering schedule so the children can take turns caring for the ants.

*If you decide to develop a list of ant words, for this activity start with the word **ant**. The children will enjoy coming up with words that rhyme with ant.*

Session 1: The Ant Hunt

What You Need

For the group

- ❏ 1 tray with a small mound of earth
- ❏ Moist food for ants (use extremely small amounts) such as canned cat or dog food, lunch meat, a piece of fruit, or a piece of sticky candy
- ❏ 1 board, log, or flat stone, such as a flagstone, approximately 8" x 12"

optional
- ❏ Several spray bottles filled with water (only if the ground outside is dry)

Getting Ready

Several Days Before the Activity

1. If you have more than six children in your group, plan to have one adult volunteer to assist with each group of four to six youngsters when you take them for a walk to look for ants, anthills, and ant trails. If the children are in small groups, they can observe the ants closely with less chance of stepping on them.

2. Look around the building for ants and around the yard or neighborhood for ants and anthills. If you can't find ants, leave something moist, such as cat or dog food, a small piece of fruit, or a piece of sticky candy outside to attract them.

3. Tell your volunteers where to take the children to find the best places for observing ants.

Anytime Before the Activity

1. Read Background Information starting on page 75.

2. Shape the pile of earth on the tray into a small mound with a hole in the top to resemble an anthill.

The Ant Hunt

1. Show the children the mound of earth. Ask, "What animal do you think could crawl through this tiny hole to its underground home?"

2. Ask, "Where have you seen ants?" "What were they doing?"

3. If the children mention seeing ants in their homes, ask, "Why do you think most people don't want ants in their homes?" "What can you do to keep them out of your home?" If the children don't know, tell them that washing cat and dog food dishes after their pet has finished eating and keeping cookie crumbs off the floor help keep ants out of their homes, because ants generally don't stay if they can't find food to eat.

4. Take the children for a walk to look for ants, anthills, and ant trails.

5. In an area where you find ants, put a board, log, or stone on the ground in hope the ants will build tunnels and chambers underneath. If the ants do dig tunnels and chambers, some of them will be on the surface of the ground where the children will see them. If the earth is dry, let the youngsters take turns making it damp as ants prefer moist soil in order to dig their tunnels. If the ants decide to tunnel where you moisten, it can take up to a week to see any tunneling activity.

6. Have the children leave tiny amounts of food for the ants under the board and on the ground near the board.

7. Tell the children they will return regularly to dampen the soil and to see what the ants are doing.

8. On the way back to the classroom, encourage the children to look around the sides of the building for ants.

9. Back in the classroom, ask questions to encourage the children to talk about what they found.
   - Where did you see ants on the walk? [in trees and on the ground near the food]
   - What color were the ants?
   - What were the ants doing?
   - Where did you see ants on our way back to the building? [along the side of the building and on the sidewalk]
   - Where did you find ants indoors? [on the floor, near the sink, and near the wall]

10. If you or the children see ants in your classroom, put the food in places where the ants can't get to it. Watch what happens. In Activity 3, when the children learn how and why ants make trails, you can remind them of this experience and ask, "Why do you think the ants left our classroom?"

Going Further

1. Encourage the children to draw or paint several pictures of ants. As an assessment tool, keep one drawing or painting from each child. At the end of this unit, have the youngsters make more drawings and ask them to describe their art work. Compare the first drawing or painting with the recent one to help assess how much your students have learned.

2. During the next several days and weeks, return to the board, log, or stone the class placed on the ground to see if ants dug tunnels and chambers underneath. If the children see ant eggs, baby ants (larvae), cocoons, and newly hatched ants in the chambers, continue to return and encourage your students to observe the development of the young ants. This will prepare them for Activity 4 where they learn about the ant life cycle.

Some teachers wipe the ant trail with a soapy sponge or put vinegar on the trail. This may kill the ants and brings up a dilemma worth discussing. It is important for children to know that even though ants are interesting creatures and it's fun to learn about them, there are places, such as our homes and classrooms, where they are not wanted. Searching for the point of entrance of the ant trail and sealing it is another way of discouraging ants from coming inside without killing them.

If you lift the stone or wood early in the day before the sun warms the ground or in the evening, you'll probably see only empty tunnels and chambers. If you lift the stone or wood during the warmest part of the day, you may see ants, eggs, larvae, cocoons, and newly hatched young in depressions on the surface of the ground.

3. If you find eggs, larvae, and cocoons, try this activity:

a. Take the children to the stone or wood early in the day, and have them feel the cool stone and ground around the stone. Ask, "How does the stone (or ground) feel?"

b. Gently lift the wood or stone, and let the children peek under it.

c. Take the children to the wood or stone again when the sun has warmed the ground, and have them feel the warm stone and the warm ground around the stone. Ask, "How does the stone (or ground) feel now?"

d. Gently lift the stone, and let the children peek under it. If they see eggs and baby ants ask, "Why do you think the nurse ants take the eggs and baby ants to a warm place?"

e. Encourage the children to make suggestions. Tell them nurse ants carry the eggs and baby ants to a warm place so the eggs will hatch sooner and the babies grow faster.

Session 2: The Ant Farm

What You Need

For the group

- ❏ 10–12 live ants (If you have ants in your area that are too large to squeeze through the cracks in an ant farm, collect them. If not, you can purchase ants. See Resources on page 79.)
- ❏ 1 commercial ant farm with sand and birdseed (See Resources on page 79.)
- ❏ Several eye droppers
- ❏ 1 cup, half filled with water

optional

- ❏ 1 homemade ant farm (See the instructions for making a homemade ant farm on page 13. The books *Ant Cities* and *questions and answers about Ants* give directions for making a homemade ant farm. See the Resources on page 79.)

Getting Ready

1. If you decide to order ants, order them several weeks before beginning the ant unit.

2. Before setting up the ant farm, carefully read the instructions that come with it. Listed below are several things to remember to ensure a successful ant farm.

   - If you collect your own ants, take them from the same nest. Ants fight and kill ants from other colonies.
   - Remember, ants bite. When collecting them, let them crawl onto a stick. Tap the stick until the ants fall into the farm.
   - Ants are tiny animals and therefore eat tiny amounts of food. Feed them only one birdseed, a piece of leaf, a pinch of canned meat, or a tiny crumb of bread soaked in sugar water every few days. Be careful not to overfeed them.
   - Ants need water, but too much can kill them. When you set up the farm, add just enough water to dampen the earth or sand. After that, add 5-6 drops every other day.
   - Avoid shaking the farm. This causes the tunnels and chambers to collapse.

- Keep the farm out of the direct sunlight. Ants die from extreme heat or cold.
- Ants also die of old age and other natural causes. It's not unusual to find dead ants in the farm. The children will be very interested to see what the live ants do with their dead companions.

The Ant Farm

Keeping live ants in your room for the children to observe is an exciting project. In every way possible, involve the children in helping you set up the ant farm and care for the ants.

1. Show the children the empty ant farm and encourage them to describe what they see.

2. Show the group the bag of sand or earth that comes with the commercial ant farm. Let the children feel the bag. Ask, "Why do you think the ants need sand?" Tell the group they can watch the ants and see what they do with it.

3. Empty the sand into the farm.

4. Show the children the cup of water and ask, "Why do you think the ants need water?"

5. Let the children take turns filling the eye droppers in the cup of water and dampening the sand. If you have a large class, you may prefer to ask for a few volunteers to add water to the ant farm. The sand needs to be evenly damp with no standing water. Too much water can cause mold.

6. Add the ants to the ant farm.

7. Let one child drop one birdseed into the farm to feed the ants.

8. Tell the children they can watch the ants but not to move the ant home. Tell them the ants may do something interesting if they aren't disturbed. (You may decide to tape the Ant Farm to a table or counter so that the children can't jiggle it.)

9. Let the children help you set up a feeding and watering schedule so they can take turns caring for the ants.

A Homemade Ant Farm

Commercial ant farms are designed to provide excellent opportunities for students to observe ant behavior. It is also fun for children to make their own farm. Follow the steps below to make a simple ant farm.

    a. Collect a small, clear cup with a lid.

    b. Use a push pin or needle to punch a few tiny holes in the lid.

    c. When you go on the ant hunt with the children, take the cup and lid.

    d. Use the cup to gently scoop up earth and at least a dozen ants. Fill the cup halfway and tightly cover it with the lid.

    e. Back in the classroom, place the cup in a pan of water, which will discourage the ants from climbing out. When the ants settle down and start tunnelling, you can remove the lid.

    f. Care for the ants following the same instructions listed under Getting Ready on page 11.

    g. Enjoy watching the ants in their new home. Carefully lift up the cup and let the children look for tunnels and chambers underneath.

    h. When the class has finished observing the ants, return the ants to their original home.

Activity 2: Ants and Ant Tunnels

Overview

Students concentrate on the ant's body structure and tunneling behavior in this activity. In Session 1: A Closer Look at Ants, the children count the ant's body parts and learn more about ants as they observe an Ant Poster. They make their own paper ants, which become part of a classroom ant society. While playing with their paper ants, the youngsters often remember and act out real animal behavior. As they play, they often create their own dramas, which encourages language development, and later, creative writing.

In Session 2: Ant Tunnels, the youngsters become familiar with the tunneling activity of ants by observing live ants digging tunnels in the ant farm. The children observe the Ant Tunnels section of the Ant Nest poster in which many ants work together digging tunnels and chambers. The boys and girls experience the darkness and confinement of a tunnel by pretending to be ants crawling through a tunnel-like structure. The class begins an ant nest mural and each child adds a paper chamber and two tunnels to the large sheet of paper.

In Making a Paper Ant (on page 17) you have a choice. You can have the children design their own ant or you can use the ant model patterns. If you have the children use the patterns, do the Getting Ready section and follow all the steps in Making a Paper Ant. Whichever approach you choose, collect the paper ants at the end for use in a later activity.

If you developed a list of ant words, for this activity add the words **tunnel, room,** *and* **chamber.**

A good way to assess what your students learned about ants is to ask the parents if their children play with their ants and create ant dramas at home. Also, ask what types of real ant behavior they act out in the dramas.

Session 1: A Closer Look at Ants

What You Need

For the group

- ❑ 1 Ant poster (page 19 and as an 11" x 17" perforated fold-out sheet in the back of this book)
- ❑ Ant model patterns—not needed if the children design their own ant (page 20 and as a perforated sheet in the back of this book)
    - ❑ Pattern A (worker ant)
    - ❑ Pattern B (ant leg)
    - ❑ Pattern C (ant antenna)

❏ 1 tray
❏ 1 large pair of scissors
❏ Newspaper (to cover the tray and work tables)

For each child and yourself
❏ 1 sheet of 6" x 6" brown construction paper (or paper from a grocery bag)
❏ 1 container of white paste or glue, or a glue stick
❏ 1 pencil or black marker
optional
> ❏ Scissors—needed if the children design their own ants
> ❏ Scraps of brown paper

Getting Ready

Anytime Before the Activity

1. Use the patterns to cut ants out of brown paper.
   - Use pattern A to cut out one ant body for each child and yourself.
   - Use patterns B and C to cut out six legs and two antennae for each ant.

2. If your children are unable to write their own names, write the children's names on the ant bodies.

Immediately Before the Activity

1. Place one paper ant body, six legs, two antennae, one pencil, paste, and newspaper on a tray. Put this tray and the ant poster in the area where you show the poster and discuss making the paper ant.

2. Spread newspaper on the tables and place one ant body, six legs, one pencil, and paste at each child's work place.

3. Have the antennae for the children's ants near the work area to distribute when the youngsters are ready for them.

Looking at the Ant Poster

1. Show the Ant Poster to the group. Have the children take turns pointing to the ant's head, legs, mouth, and feelers. (Instead of the words *mouth* and *feelers*, use the words *jaws* and *antennae*, if you think they are appropriate for your group.)

2. Count the two antennae and ask, "How do you think ants use their feelers?" [for touch, smell, and possibly for hearing]

3. Along with the children, count the ant's six legs. Show them the claws on the ends of the ant's legs. Ask, "Why do ants have these on their legs?" [to help them climb]

4. Have a child point to the ant's two large eyes. Tell the class that some ants have three tiny eyes on the top of their head. Have the child point to those eyes and count them.

5. Ask, "How many major body parts are on the ant?" Start with the head and count the three parts. For older children, name the three major parts as you count: *head*, *thorax* (the middle section), *abdomen*.

Making a Paper Ant

1. Have the children make their own ants.

Child-Designed Ant
- If the children have the necessary skills, let them design, cut out, and assemble their own ants. These ants may be somewhat realistic or very imaginative. The purpose of this approach is to encourage the children's creativity and self-initiated work.

Making an Ant Model
- The process of assembling precut ant parts encourages the children to think about the parts of a real ant as they make an ant with three body sections, six legs, two antennae, eyes, and possibly jaws. Although structured, it allows for individual expression in the placement of the body parts. You will find no two ants made by the children ever look exactly alike.

  a. Put the tray on the floor in the discussion area so the children can see it. Let the children help you make a paper ant.

  b. Show them the ant body cutout. Ask, "Which end of the ant do you think is the head, the bigger or the smaller end?" [the smaller end]

  c. Have a child point to the head.

  d. Ask, "What does the ant need on its head?" [eyes, mouth, feelers] Draw five eyes and a mouth, and glue two feelers onto the head.

  e. Ask, "What else does the ant need?" [legs]

To reinforce the idea ants have three body sections, you may want to precut paper into three rectangles for each child to use as a starting point in designing their own ant. If you do this, the children will need scraps of brown paper for cutting out legs, antennae, and jaws.

The teacher demonstration of building an ant model is a good way to review ideas about ant body structure. It is not meant to make any child feel they did something "incorrect."

    f. Have the children count the legs as you glue six legs onto the thorax, the middle body section.

    g. When the youngsters are ready to glue the antennae onto their ants, have the children use the words *feelers* or **antennae** to ask for them.

    h. If the children ask to make jaws for their ants, give them the scraps of brown paper and scissors.

2. Have the children go to the work tables and, if they can write their own names, have them write their names on the ant bodies.

3. Collect the children's paper ants for use in Session 3: The Ant Mural. Tell the children to leave their ants at school because in a later class they will make a home for their ants.

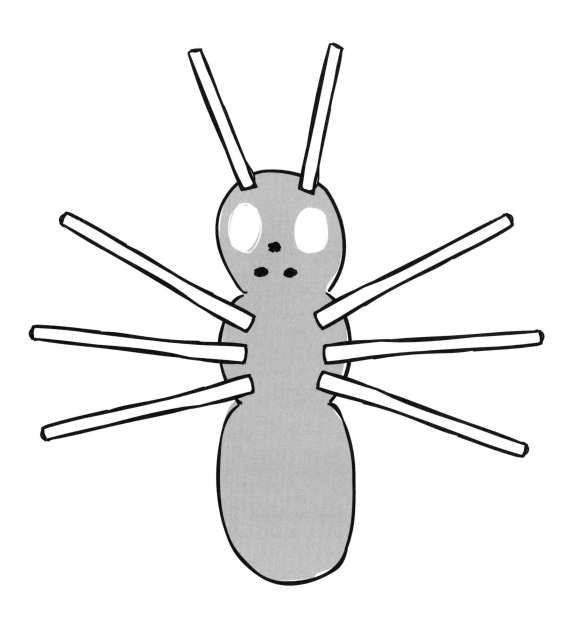

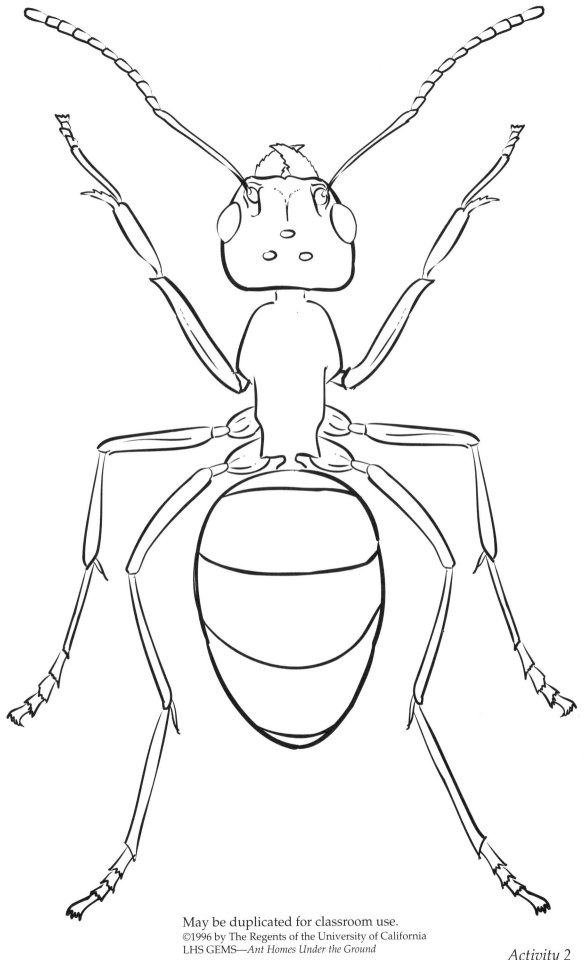

May be duplicated for classroom use.
©1996 by The Regents of the University of California
LHS GEMS—*Ant Homes Under the Ground*

Activity 2   **19**

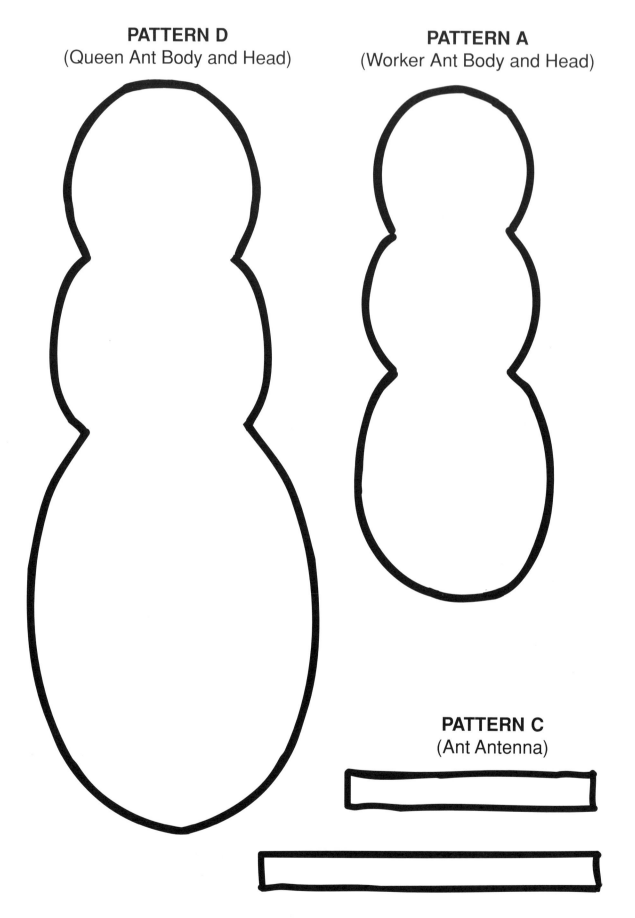

PATTERN D
(Queen Ant Body and Head)

PATTERN A
(Worker Ant Body and Head)

PATTERN C
(Ant Antenna)

PATTERN B
(Ant Leg)

May be duplicated for classroom use.
©1996 by The Regents of the University of California
LHS GEMS—*Ant Homes Under the Ground*

Session 2: Ant Tunnels

What You Need

For the group

- ❏ 1 Ant Farm
- ❏ Sections 1 and 2 of the Ant Nest poster—Ant Tunnels
  (The sections are 11" x 17" perforated fold-out sheets in the
  back of this unit.)
- ❏ Several ant books with good pictures of tunnels.
  (See Resources on page 79.)
- ❏ 1 or 2 tunnels made from sheets or blankets draped over
  chairs or tables; or use a commercial tunnel (a fabric-
  covered spiral large enough for a child to crawl through—
  available at many toy stores)
- ❏ 1 chamber made from a table with a blanket or sheet thrown
  over it; or use a tent or a large box, such as a box a refrigera-
  tor or oven is shipped in. Connect the chamber to the
  tunnel(s).
- ❏ Ant Farm Activity Sheet (page 24 and as a perforated sheet
  in the back of this unit)

Getting Ready

*Some teachers laminate the posters
to make it easier to remove the tape
so they can use the posters again.*

Anytime Before the Activity

Tape together Sections 1
and 2 (Ant Tunnels) of the
Ant Nest poster as
shown here.

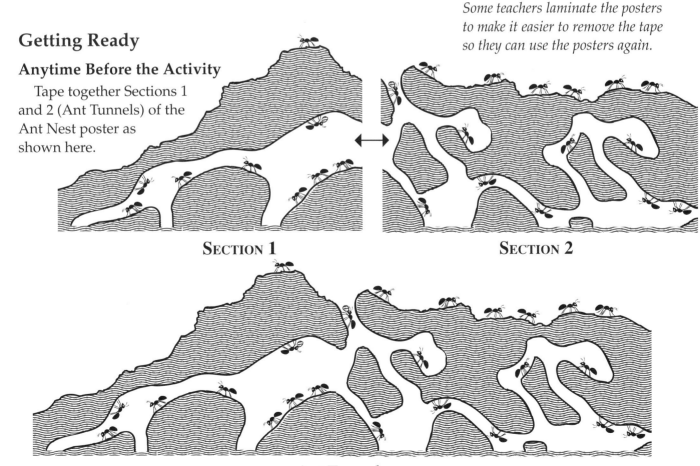

SECTION 1 ↔ **SECTION 2**

Ant Tunnels

The Ant Farm

1. Encourage the children to observe the tunneling activities of the ants in the ant farm.

2. Allow time for the children to tell some of the things they saw the ants doing.

Tunnels

1. Show the children the Ant Tunnels sections of the poster. Ask, "What do you think the ants are doing?" Tell the children ants use the tunnels and rooms as the children use hallways and rooms in their own homes. If appropriate for your group, tell the class that the rooms are called *chambers.*

2. Have the children compare the different ways people and ants dig tunnels. Ask, "Have you ever dug a tunnel in damp sand?" "What did you use?" [hands, shovel] Ask, "When an ant digs tunnels, what does it use to pick up little pieces of sand or dirt and carry them out of the nest?" [its mouth]

3. Let the children role-play ants crawling through the tunnel(s) and in and out of the chamber you made with the blankets and/or sheets.

4. Keep the ant books in the room so the children can look at them as often as they like.

5. Hang the combined Sections 1 and 2 (Ant Tunnels) portion of the Ant Nest poster in a place where the children can look at it often.

For Kindergarten and First Grade

1. Have a child use a finger to trace the tunnels in the ant farm. Introduce the Ant Farm Activity Sheet. Give each child an activity sheet. The children can use a pencil, crayon, or marker to draw ants and ant tunnels on their sheets. Kindergartners can draw tunnels and ants any way they wish. Encourage first graders to try and draw the tunnels similar to the ones the live ants made. If they record the date on their sheets and then make new activity sheets in the future, they can compare the changes that have taken place in the Ant Farm.

2. Post one or more completed activity sheets next to the Ant Farm. You may wish to have more blank activity sheets available so your students can record new tunnels in the future.

Going Further

1. Encourage the children to use their hands, spoons, or shovels to dig tunnels and chambers in damp sand. They can play with plastic ants and ant food, such as plastic grasshoppers and beetles, in the tunnels.

2. Children enjoy playing with their paper ants, making them crawl in and out of three-dimensional chambers and tunnels. Collect several brown cardboard boxes, especially long rectangular ones. Tape down the loose pieces of the boxes and cut openings in their ends large enough for the children to fit their hands and paper ants through. Let the children play freely with their paper ants and the cardboard-box tunnels and chambers.

Ant Farm Activity Sheet

May be duplicated for classroom use.
©1996 by The Regents of the University of California
LHS GEMS—*Ant Homes Under the Ground*

Session 3: The Ant Nest Mural

As a class project, students construct an Ant Nest mural consisting of a network of connecting chambers and tunnels, filled with ants, ant food, and possibly eggs, larvae, and pupae. Since each child likes to take home his or her paper ant and ant nest at the end of the unit, the mural is designed so each child first makes an individual nest and then attaches it to the large class mural. Each child fills the individual nest and, if you wish, they can later detach it from the large mural and take it home.

The mural allows flexibility for different approaches. The children can make individual nests (tunnels and chambers) and not work on a class mural. Or, they can make individual nests and place their nests on the large mural, which can be taken apart later so the children can take their creations home.

The purpose of this session is to help children understand that ants work together to build tunnels to connect all the chambers inside an ant nest. By using precut tunnels and chambers (all of similar size), the children can work together to make their tunnels connect with their classmate's tunnels. Later the children fill their chambers with colorful and imaginative surprises.

What You Need

For a group of 10-12 children
- ❏ 1 large piece of butcher paper (about 3' x 10')
- ❏ Several paper ants

For each child and yourself
- ❏ 1 sheet of butcher paper (18" x 18")
- ❏ 2 sheets of gray or white construction paper (9" x 12")
- ❏ 1 marker or pencil
- ❏ 1 container of glue

Getting Ready

1. For each child and yourself, precut the two sheets of gray construction paper.
   - Cut one sheet in half lengthwise into two 4 ½" x 12" strips.
   - Cut the other to resemble an ant chamber. (See the drawing on page 26.)

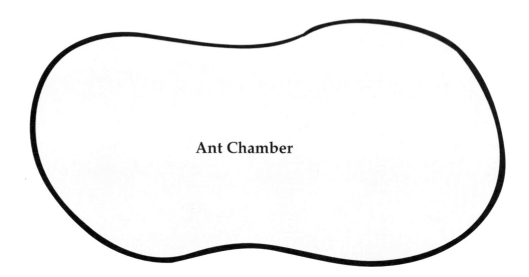

Ant Chamber

The Ant Nest Mural Drama

1. While the children are sitting on the floor in front of the mural, use the paper ants, a chamber, and tunnel to present a short drama of ants tunneling in the ground. Tell a story such as the following.
    -   Let's pretend this brown sheet of paper is the ground.
    -   This ant wants to make its home under the ground. What can it do? [dig a tunnel]
    -   It begins to dig. (Lay down the paper tunnel. Put the ant in the tunnel.)
    -   Other ants join in to help it dig. (Put more ants in the tunnel.)
    -   They dig a chamber. (Lay down the paper chamber and put the ants in it.)

2. Give each child one tunnel and one chamber. Let the children take turns placing them on the mural to continue the drama. Encourage them to try and place the tunnels and chambers on the mural so each tunnel connects to another tunnel or chamber. This will give the group an idea of what the finished mural may look like.

3. After the drama, pick up the paper chambers and tunnels but leave the mural paper on the floor for the next activity.

Beginning the Mural

1. Show the group the small sheet of butcher paper and explain that each child will make his or her own chamber and attach two tunnels. Write your name on the paper and glue on the chamber and two tunnels.

2. At the tables, have each child glue a chamber and two tunnels on a sheet of paper.

3. Let the children arrange their pictures on the large mural, trying to make the tunnels connect. Tape the pictures to the mural or leave them unattached. Caution the youngsters to walk around the mural so they won't step on the ant nest.

4. Let the children place their paper ants on the mural.

5. Tell the girls and boys to leave their ants and ant homes at school because they will make more things to add to the mural.

Activity 3: What Happens Inside an Ant's Home?

Overview

The emphasis in this activity is on ant food. The children learn about the variety of foods ants eat, how ants move the food, and where they put it inside their nest.

In Session 1: Scouts and Guards, the girls and boys pretend to be scout ants in an anthill. They follow a scent trail to a bag of crackers and carry the crackers back to an anthill to share. As "guard ants," several children stand at the entrance to the nest, protecting the nest from "enemy ants" by checking the scent of the "ants" that enter.

In Session 2: Dragging Food into the Nest, cooperative problem solving is encouraged as four children work together to move a large and awkward "caterpillar" across the room and into a "tunnel." The problem of how to fit a large object into a relatively small enclosed space challenges the children to decide whether to carry, push, or pull it through the tunnel. Teamwork, as with ants, is necessary to accomplish this task.

*If you developed a list of ant words, for this activity add the words **caterpillar, grasshopper, cracker, scout ant, guard ant,** and **housekeeper ant.***

While observing the Ant Nest poster in Session 3: More Ant Food, the children discover a caterpillar and a grasshopper in the ant nest. They also see scout ants leaving the nest to look for food, guard ants protecting the nest, and housekeeper ants dragging dead ants away as they clean their home. The youngsters go outside to check the ant food and add an unusual morsel to their ant farm.

Session 1: Scouts and Guards

What You Need

For the drama
- ❑ 1 brown towel, sheet, or blanket
- ❑ 1 bucket
- ❑ 1 doll
- ❑ 1 lunch bag
- ❑ 1 graham cracker
- ❑ Several paper ants made in the last activity

For the group

- ❏ 1 bottle of lemon or strawberry extract, or any familiar food extract with a mild scent (Use this scent in Following the Scent Trail on page 32.)
- ❏ 1 bottle of peppermint extract, or any familiar food extract with a strong scent (Use this scent in Guarding the Nest on page 33.)
- ❏ 2 plastic bags for cotton balls
- ❏ 1 piece of string or thick yarn approximately 10 yards long, for an ant trail (Could use a chalk line on cement.)
- ❏ 1 grocery bag
- ❏ 1 tray
- ❏ Several extra cotton balls

For each child and yourself

- ❏ 1 cracker
- ❏ 1 cotton ball

Getting Ready

Immediately Before the Activity

1. Choose a place for a child-size anthill, either a section of the classroom, a whole room, or an outdoor area such as a large sandbox or a domed climbing structure. Put the tray in the "anthill."

The purpose of the string is to define the trail and make it easier for the children to follow it.

2. Make an ant trail by tying the string to some object in the "anthill" and extending it along the ground to a paper bag containing one cracker for each child and one for yourself. If you use a room as the "anthill," the trail can lead outdoors or down a hallway.

3. When preparing both the cotton balls with the mild scent and those with the strong scent, do the following.
   a. Mix four teaspoons of food extract with four tablespoons of water.
   b. Pour the mixture over the cotton balls.
   c. Squeeze the excess liquid out of the cotton balls. Put them in a plastic bag and place the bag near the anthill.

Setting Up for the Drama

1. Put several paper ants inside the bucket.

2. Wrap the towel around the bucket to create a pretend anthill. Leave an opening on top so you can take the ants out and put them back in the anthill.

3. Put the doll on the floor near the anthill. Place the paper bag on her lap with the cracker in her hand.

The Scout Ants Drama

1. Present a drama to introduce the idea that an ant dabs scent from the end of its abdomen to leave a scent trail for other ants to follow. Use the doll, the children's paper ants, the pretend anthill, a lunch bag, and a cracker to dramatize the following story.

   - A little girl named Kimi is sitting outside one day eating a snack.
   - Kimi says, "I don't want to eat this cracker. I'll leave it in my lunch bag and take a nap." (Make Kimi put the cracker in the bag and lie down.)
   - While Kimi sleeps, look what is happening nearby. (Make an ant climb out of the anthill, walk toward the bag, and crawl inside.)
   - What do you think the ant is doing?
   - The hungry ant finds the cracker. It carries a small piece of the cracker in its mouth. (Break off a piece of cracker and hold it next to the ant's mouth.)
   - As it walks back to the anthill, it dabs the end of its body (abdomen) on the ground. (Dab end of abdomen on ground.) Why do you think it does that?
   - The ant is leaving a smell (scent) on the ground so other ants can find the food. (Have the ant carry the cracker into the anthill and disappear.)
   - Look what's happening! Other ants are using their antennae to smell. (Make several ants walk single-file from the anthill to the bag, dabbing their antennae on the ground.) They have found the scent.
   - They find the cracker and carry parts of it to the anthill. (Make the ants return to the anthill with a piece of cracker, then disappear inside.)
   - Kimi wakes up. (Have her sit up and stretch.) She says, "I'm hungry. I'll eat my cracker." (Have her look in the bag, then turn to the class and ask, "Where is it?")

For older students, the drama can be done without the doll. Put the cracker on a table and have the scout ants leave the anthill and hunt for food. They can find the cracker left over from a picnic.

2. Ask, "What do you think the ants that find food are called?" Accept all suggestions, such as hunter ants, but tell the group that they are usually known as *scout ants*.

3. Ask a few review questions such as:
   - How did the scout ants tell the other ants where the crackers were? [they left a scent trail]
   - What part of the ant's body did it use to help it find the scent? [antennae]

4. Leave the doll, paper ants, "anthill," bag, and cracker out so the children can continue to play with them.

Following the Scent Trail

1. Have the children sit with you inside the child-size "anthill." Tell the group to pretend that everyone inside the anthill is an ant and all the ants are hungry.

Some teachers encourage their students to wear paper antennae during Following the Scent Trail to reinforce the idea that ants smell with their antennae. The children can touch the ground with their paper antennae as they crawl along the trail.

2. Tell the children they can pretend to be scout ants like the ants in the drama. As scout ants, they need to leave a scent trail when they bring food back to the anthill, so other ants can follow the smell. The smell comes out of the ant's body.

3. Pass around one of the scented cotton balls for the children to smell. Say, "This is the special smell of all the ants that live in our anthill."

4. Tell the children they will follow a trail to food and will leave their special smell on the trail.

5. Show the children how to leave a scent trail by following the string trail to the paper bag. Take one cracker out of the bag and carry it back to the "anthill," while dabbing the cotton ball on the trail.

6. Place the cracker on the tray. Tell the children you are pretending the tray is a special room (*chamber*) in the anthill where the ants store their food.

7. Tell the children that each "ant" will bring a cracker back to the "anthill" and store it in this special room. Then all the "ants" will eat the crackers.

8. Give one scented cotton ball to each child.

9. Have each child take a turn dabbing scent on the trail while bringing a cracker back to the "anthill" to place on the tray. Once each child has had a turn, the whole class can share the crackers.

10. Save the cotton balls to use in Guarding the Nest.

Guarding the Nest

1. Tell the class that an ant nest is sometimes attacked by ants from another nest. Ask, "Why would ants from one ant nest try to get into another ant nest?" [to get food] "What do you think ants could do to protect their nest?" [bite, sting]

2. Ask, "What do you think the ants protecting the nest are called?" Accept all suggestions, such as soldier ants or police ants, but tell the children that they are usually known as *guard ants*.

3. Ask, "How do you think guard ants know that an ant is from another nest?" [by its smell, its scent] Ask, "What do ants have to help them smell other ants?" [antennae]

4. Choose several students to be guard ants and have them stand at the entrance to the "anthill" with their cotton balls.

5. Have the rest of the class stand outside the "anthill" with their cotton balls.

6. Without the guard ants seeing you, select several children to be ants from a different nest. Take away the mild-scented cotton balls and give them the strongly scented cotton balls (a scent that is different from nest scent).

7. Ask the guard ants, "What will you do if ants with a different smell try to enter your nest?" [not let them in] Tell the guard ants this is a friendly game and they should politely tell the other ants they can't come in.

8. As each child approaches the nest entrance, tell the guard ants to sniff the ant's cotton ball for the nest scent before letting the ant enter. To help the guard ants decided which ants to let in, have them smell their own cotton ball and compare its scent with the scent of the cotton ball of the ant trying to enter the "anthill."

Use the stronger scent in Guarding the Nest so the guard ants can distinguish the smell of the invading ants from the scent of their nest.

Session 2: Dragging Food into the Nest

What You Need

For the group

- ❏ 1 or 2 tunnels made from sheets or blankets draped over tables; or use a commercial tunnel (a fabric-covered spiral large enough for a child to crawl through)
- ❏ 1 sleeping bag, blanket, or bedspread to make a caterpillar; or 1 large pillow or cushion to make a bug
- ❏ 4 pieces of rope or strips of fabric, 2' long, for the "caterpillar"

optional
- ❏ 2 round fabric "eyes," about 3" in diameter
- ❏ 1 needle and thread for sewing eyes onto the "caterpillar" or "bug"

Getting Ready

Anytime Before the Activity

Make a "caterpillar" by rolling the sleeping bag, blanket, or bedspread lengthwise and tying ropes or strips of fabric around it.

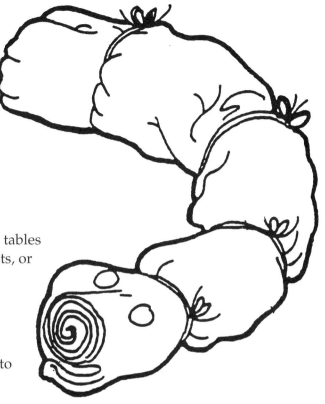

> *optional*
> Sew the eyes onto the "caterpillar" or "bug."

Immediately Before the Activity

Make a tunnel in a room or outside by pushing tables together and covering them with sheets or blankets, or use a commercial tunnel.

Dragging Food into the Nest

1. When the children arrive, allow time for them to crawl in and out of the tunnel. Ask, "What animals crawl in tunnels?" [snakes, moles, worms, rabbits, ants] "Why do they crawl in tunnels?" [to stay safe, to rest, to eat their food]

2. Gather the group together in a circle on the floor and ask, "What do ants eat?" Tell the children ants eat dead beetles, butterflies, grasshoppers, and caterpillars, as well as crackers.

3. Ask the children if they have ever seen ants carrying a caterpillar or some other food that was much larger than the ants. Ask, "What did you see them do with the food?"

4. Drag the pretend caterpillar over to the circle and say to the group, "Ants sometimes need to carry very large food into a tunnel. Pretend you are ants and try to move this caterpillar through our tunnel."

5. Have the children crawl across the room, in groups of four, carrying the caterpillar. Encourage them to work together to move the caterpillar through the tunnel. They can pretend the tunnel leads to a food chamber where they can store the caterpillar.

6. Have the children sit down and talk about dragging the cater-pillar through the tunnel. Ask questions to encourage them to talk about what they did and how it felt.
   - What did you do to move the caterpillar?
   - How did you help your friends?
   - How did you feel when you were moving the caterpillar through the tunnel?

7. Leave the caterpillar and tunnel out in a free play area for the children to play with later.

Going Further

For older students, you may want to provide more information to help them understand how strong ants are. An ant can carry many times its own weight. Gather the children around a desk or heavy table and tell them that if they were ants they could easily carry the desk or table.

Session 3: More Ant Food

What You Need

For the group
- ❑ 1 Ant Farm
- ❑ Ant Nest poster (The sections are 11" x 17" perforated fold-out sheets in the back of this unit.)
- ❑ 1 roll of clear tape
- ❑ 1 roll of masking tape, or push pins
- ❑ 1 tiny scrap of food, such as a dead gnat or about a ¹⁄₁₆" slice of strawberry
- ❑ Markers or crayons in assorted colors

optional
- ❑ Several spray bottles filled with water

Getting Ready

Anytime Before the Activity
1. Tape together sections 3 and 4 of the Ant Nest poster (Ant Food) and connect it to the bottom of sections 1 and 2 (Ant Tunnels) to make a complete Ant Nest poster (see page 37).

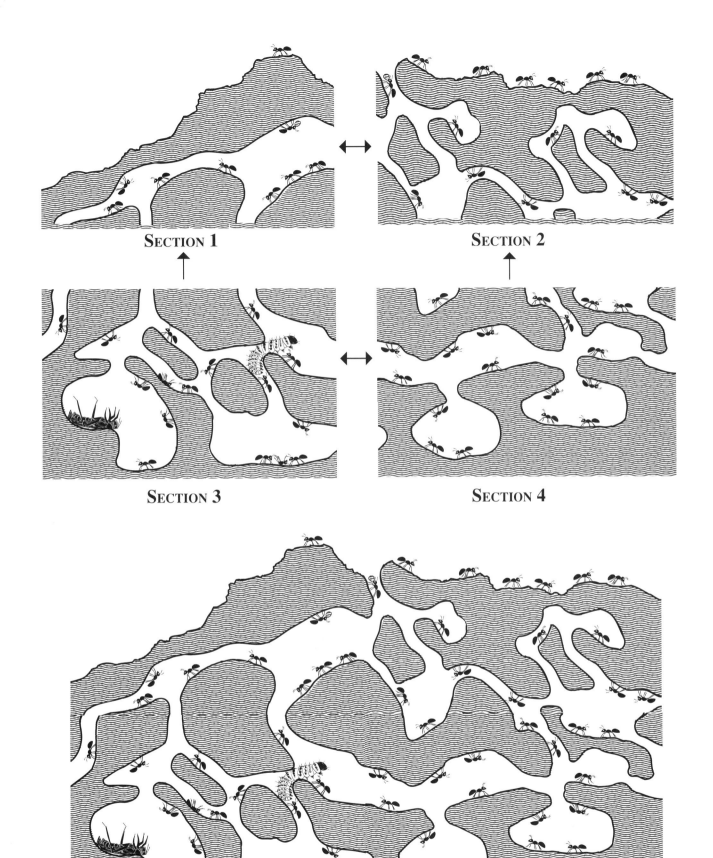

Section 1

Section 2

Section 3

Section 4

ANT NEST

2. Use the crayons or markers to color the caterpillar on the poster.

3. Use the masking tape or push pins to hang the poster in a place where the children will notice it and have time to observe it closely.

The Ant Walk

1. Now that the children know about ant trails, what ants eat, and how ants carry insects much larger than themselves, the students probably will be much more observant and interested in seeing what the live ants ate. Take the class outside to check the food left near and under the board or stone (placed there in Activity 1) to see if any food is missing or if anything else has changed.

2. If the ground is dry, let the children take turns dampening it with the spray bottles of water.

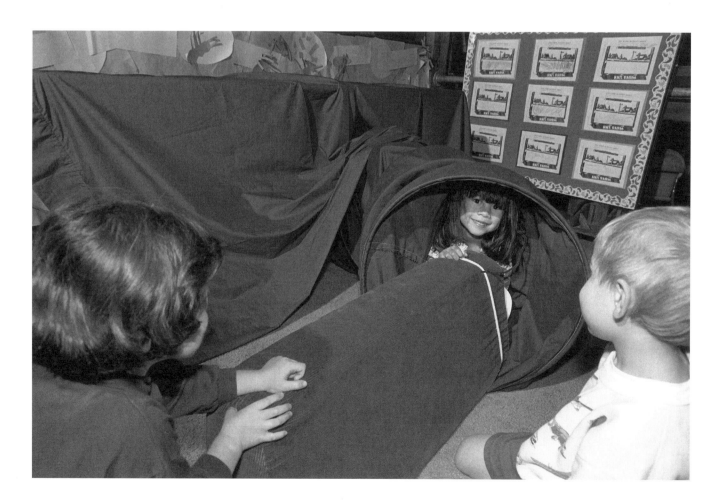

The Ant Farm

Since the youngsters are now familiar with a variety of foods ants eat, they may want to feed their ants something different. Let a child drop a tiny piece of fruit or a gnat into the ant farm so the whole class can observe what happens.

The Ant Food Poster

1. Before the class begins, encourage the children to look at the Ant Nest poster.

2. Gather a few children at a time in front of the poster and ask, "What are the ants doing now?"

3. Ask a child to point to the room with the grasshopper. Ask, "Why do you think a grasshopper is in the ant nest?" [ants eat dead grasshoppers]

4. Ask a child to find the scout ants leaving the nest to look for food.

5. Ask a child to point to the two ants at the top of the ant nest, outside the entrance. Tell the group these ants are protecting the nest. Ask, "What do you think they are called?" [guard ants]

6. Introduce the concept of *housekeeper ants* by telling the group that some ants, called housekeeper ants, have the job of dragging rotten food, even dead ants, out of the nest to keep the ant home clean. Ask, "Why do you think these ants are called that?" [because they keep the ant house clean] Acknowledge all responses in a positive way. Have a child point to an ant that is dragging a dead ant out of the nest.

One teacher assigned "ant jobs" to the children in her class; the "scout ants" carried snacks to the tables and the "housekeeper ants" cleaned the tables after snacks. Encourage a feeling of cooperation in your classroom by thinking of ant jobs your students can do to help.

For Kindergarten and First Grade

Write the words Scout Ants, Guard Ants, and Housekeeper Ants on the board or word cards to familiarize your students with them.

40

Activity 4: How Ants Grow and Change

Overview

The children are introduced to the life cycle of ants in this activity. They discover the queen ant in a chamber on the Ant Nest poster. They learn the queen ant lays all the eggs and nurse ants take care of the eggs and baby ants. They also learn about other jobs ants do as part of the ant community.

As the children decide what jobs they want their paper ants to do, they expand the Ant Nest mural by adding paper food, eggs, and baby ants. The children begin to realize it takes many different workers doing many different jobs to keep an ant nest and society functioning.

If you developed a list of ant words, for this activity add the words **queen ant, eggs,** *and* **nurse ant.**

A Choice in Presenting Activity 4

The changes that occur during the ant's life cycle may be difficult for preschoolers and kindergartners to understand, especially the idea of change during the pupal stage. For four- and five-year-olds, you may decide not to do the complete life cycle section, starting on page 44 entitled For First Grade. Without discussing the specific stages in the ant's life cycle, you can tell young children that baby ants grow bigger and change into grown-up ants.

What You Need

For the group

- ❏ Ant Nest mural with the children's individual nests from Activity 2, Session 3
- ❏ Paper ants made in Activity 2, Session 1
- ❏ 1 sheet of 6" x 8" brown construction paper (or paper from a grocery bag) for the queen ant
- ❏ Patterns B , C, and D (queen ant) on page 20
- ❏ Ant Nest poster
- ❏ Section 5 (Queen and Eggs) of the Ant Nest poster (The section is an 11" x 17" perforated fold-out in the back of this book.)
- ❏ 1 Ant Farm
- ❏ 1 paper chamber
- ❏ 1 paper tunnel
- ❏ 1 roll of masking tape or several push pins
- ❏ 1 roll of clear tape

❏ Scraps of white, green, yellow, and brown paper
❏ Several white crayons
❏ Markers or crayons in assorted colors
❏ Several containers of glue or glue sticks
❏ Several scissors
❏ Several ant books with good pictures of ant eggs and larvae
   (See Resources on page 79.)

optional

❏ Section 6 (Larvae and Pupae) of the Ant Nest poster
   (The section is a 11" x 17" perforated fold-out
   in the back of this unit.)

Getting Ready

1. Ask a child to make one queen ant, or make one yourself.
    a. Draw a queen ant body on brown paper and cut it out.
       Make it larger than the other ant bodies. (You can design
       your own or use the patterns on page 20.)
    b. Glue six legs onto the middle body section (thorax) of the
       queen ant body and two antennae onto the head.
    c. Draw two big eyes and three small ones on the head.

2. Use the crayons or markers to color the caterpillar on Section 6
   of the Ant Nest poster.

3. Use the clear tape or push pins to overlay the Queen and Eggs
   section onto the Ant Nest poster. Place it in the bottom left
   corner completely covering that area. The tunnels and
   chambers are exactly the same, but something in them has
   changed. (See the drawing on the next page.)

The Ant Farm

Encourage the children to check the Ant Farm to find out what
happened to the food placed in it during the previous activity.

For Kindergarten and First Grade

Let each child draw ants, tunnels, chambers, and food on a new
Ant Farm Activity Sheet. First graders can record the date on their
sheets and compare them with the sheets they did in Activity 2.

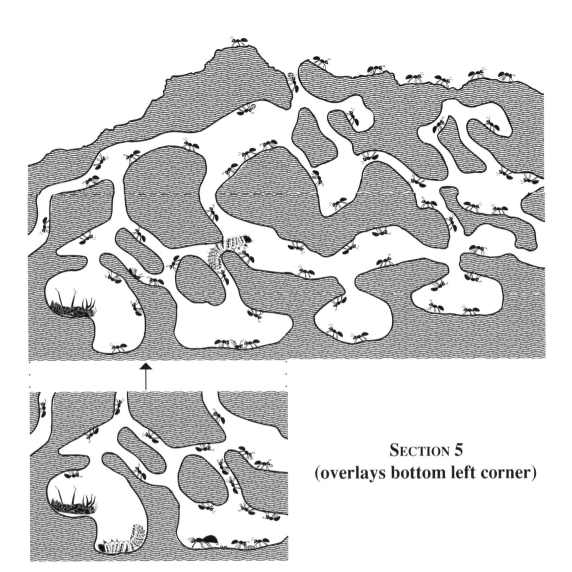

**SECTION 5
(overlays bottom left corner)**

The Queen Ant

1. Before the class begins, encourage the children to look at the Ant Nest poster to see if there are any changes.

2. Gather a small group of children in front of the poster and ask, "Do you see anything new that the ants are doing in their nest?" Allow time for the children to share their ideas. If they don't already know, tell them ants have a queen, who lays all the eggs, and the eggs are kept in special rooms (chambers).

3. Ask a child to point to the chamber with the queen and the eggs.

4. Ask, "Do you see ants carrying eggs?"

5. Have a child point to the ants carrying eggs. Tell the group that as soon as the queen lays the eggs, other ants clean them and

carry them to another chamber. Ask, "What do you think the ants that take care of the eggs are called?" [*nurse ants, baby-sitter ants*] Have a child point to a nurse ant.

6. Ask, "What do you think baby ants look like when they hatch out of eggs?" Encourage the children to imagine what the baby ants look like. After they express their ideas, tell them the baby ants that hatch from the eggs are small and white, and look like tiny worms.

7. Show pictures of ant eggs and babies from the reference books—see Resources on page 79.

8. Leave the poster on the wall until you finish all the ant activities to give the children time to refer back to it.

For First Grade

First graders, especially children who have watched meal worms change into grain beetles or caterpillars into moths or butterflies, can understand and would enjoy learning about the ant's complete life cycle from egg to adult.

1. Attach Section 6 (Larvae and Pupae) to the Ant Nest poster. (See the drawing on the next page.) Place it in the bottom right corner completely covering that part of the poster. The tunnels and chambers are exactly the same, but something in them has changed. Ask, "What do you think is happening in this picture?" Let the children express their ideas. Ask a child to point to the chamber with the baby ants. If appropriate, introduce the word *larvae.*

2. Ask, "Do you see a nurse ant taking care of the babies?" Have a child point to a nurse ant in the chamber with the babies.

3. Have a child point to a nurse ant that is carrying a baby ant. Tell the children that nurse ants often move the babies to warmer chambers.

4. Tell the group that baby ants, like caterpillars, spin *cocoons.* Ask a child to point to a cocoon. Tell the children that when the babies are in the cocoon something exciting happens. If the children don't know, tell them the baby ants stay very still and slowly turn into grown-up ants with six legs, two antennae, and three body sections. If appropriate, introduce the word *pupae.*

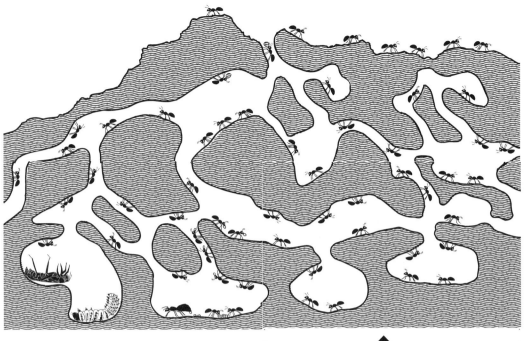

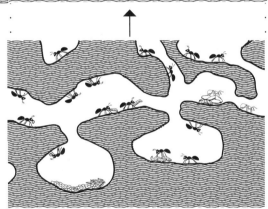

SECTION 6
(overlays bottom right corner)

5. Ask a child to point to a white ant. Tell the group that ants are white when they first come out of the cocoon. Later they get darker.

6. Review the ant's life cycle on the poster by having a child point to an egg, a tiny larva, a bigger larva, a cocoon, and a newly hatched ant.

7. Another way to review the ant's life cycle is to role play with the children the four stages of egg, larva, pupa, and adult. You can help them pretend to be:
   - An egg. (Curl up in a squatting position.)
   - A larva crawling out of the egg, eating, and growing bigger. (Pretend to crawl and eat. Stretch out to make yourself taller.)
   - A pupa. (Be very still.)
   - An adult. (Pretend to crawl away.)

The Ant Nest Mural Grows

1. With the children sitting in a circle, place one new chamber and one tunnel on the floor. Walk a child's ant and a queen ant onto the chamber. Ask the children, "Which ant do you think is the queen?" [the big one] Ask, "Why do you think she is so big?" [because she lays all the eggs, and there are many eggs inside her]

2. Pretend the queen is laying eggs. Use a white crayon to draw several eggs in the chamber.

3. Attach the new chamber and tunnel to the mural. Tape the queen ant in the chamber.

4. Let the children decide what jobs they want their ants to do and then add something new to their section of the mural. They could pretend their ants are one of the following.
   - Scout ants (add paper caterpillars, grasshoppers, or other ant food to the mural)
   - Nurse ants (add eggs, larvae, and pupae)
   - Housekeeper ants (add dead ants to be carried out of the nest)
   - Guard ants (add enemy ants trying to enter the nest)
   - Worker ants (add small pieces of mural paper at the entrance to the nest to represent a pile of dirt carried out of the nest)

5. Make available colored paper, markers or crayons, glue, and scissors so each child can add to the mural. The children can work in small groups or as a whole class. During the next few days, they may continue to add new creations to the mural.

Leave the expanded Ant Nest poster out for the children to continue to observe.

6. When the children finish the mural, the groups that made individual nests can take them and their ants home. If the students glued their chambers, tunnels, ants, ant food, and other creations directly onto the large mural, you may be able to cut the mural into pieces so each child has a piece to take home.

7. Encourage the children to play with their ants and ant nests at home and use them to create dramas for their friends and family.

For Kindergarten and First Grade

Write the words larvae and pupae on the board or word cards so that the students begin to recognize the words.

Going Further

1. Let the children role play housekeeper ants, guards, queen, nurses, babies, and scouts. You may want to have the "tunnels" and "chambers" set up for the children to crawl through.

2. Encourage the children to make an Ant Book. They can draw pictures and write or dictate stories about ants. They can include their Ant Farm Activity Sheets.

3. In a large outdoor sandbox, encourage a small group of two or three children at a time to pretend they are ants digging tunnels and chambers in the damp sand. Do this activity on a warm day when the sun is shining.

   a. Give each child several "ant eggs" (such as small rocks, preferably white and egg-shaped) and "baby ants" (such as peanut-shaped packing material) to hide in the "chambers."

   b. Have the youngsters use their hands to feel the coolness in the chambers beneath the sand and the warmth on the surface of the sand. Ask, "How does it feel under the sand?" "How does it feel on top of the sand?"

   c. Ask, "Where do you think the nurse ants would put the eggs and baby ants to keep them warm?" Encourage the children to move the "eggs" to a warm place and use a board or large piece of cardboard to cover them.

48

Activity 5: Fill the Hill

Overview

The children work with an anthill game board to reinforce their knowledge of ants and to practice important mathematics skills in this final activity. They count in context, which supports one-to-one correspondence as well as number/quantity relationships. The children do simple addition using their game boards and develop spatial-orientation and visualization-discrimination skills. Cooperative work skills are encouraged. The mathematics is in the context of real-world experiences so it has more meaning.

In Session 1, the children focus on the various jobs ants do. They are introduced to the Fill the Hill game board and the materials used to fill it—plastic ants, eggs, caterpillars, grasshoppers, and pieces of cracker. After a brief group introduction, the children are given their own set of materials to play with and explore. This is an independent activity—children spontaneously share stories and information about their anthill as they work side by side. In Session 2, they work together with a partner to again place items on the game board—this time it is a cooperative venture to prepare them for the last session of the activity. In Session 3, the children play a specially designed cooperative logic game that allows partners to collaboratively "Fill the Hill" according to the directions on a set of cards.

If you developed a list of ant words, for this activity review all the words.

*In order for kindergarten and first grade students to gain the most from this activity they need to understand the words and be able to identify **eggs, guard ant, scout ant, housekeeper ant, nurse ant, cracker, caterpillar,** and **grasshopper.***

Session 1: Introducing the Fill the Hill Game Board

What You Need

For each child and yourself

- ❏ 1 Fill the Hill game board (page 52 and an 11" x 17" perforated fold-out sheet in the back of this book)
- ❏ 1 plastic container
- ❏ 15–20 plastic ants
- ❏ 5–10 grains of uncooked rice to represent the ant eggs
- ❏ 2 one-inch pieces of green yarn to represent a grasshopper
- ❏ 2 one-inch pieces of yellow yarn to represent caterpillars

Some teachers used the largest
grains of rice available to
represent the eggs while other
teachers used small pinto beans.
Still other teachers created a
magnetic board modeled on the
game board for demonstration
purposes.

❑ 1 small piece (about half-an-inch square) of a graham or
saltine cracker

optional

❑ crayons, markers, and/or pencils

Getting Ready

Anytime Before the Activity

Duplicate one copy of the Fill the Hill game board for each child
in the class. Decide if they will keep the board at the end of the
activity to take it home to share with their families, or if you will
collect the game boards for use in Session 2. If they keep the
board, have crayons, markers, and/or pencils available for them
to fill the anthill at the end of the activity.

Just Before the Activity

1. Fill each container with the plastic ants, rice, crackers, and yarn
pieces.

2. Place the game boards and containers at tables ready for the
children to use.

Introducing the Fill the Hill Game Board

1. Gather the children in a group area away from their tables or
desks. Hold up the game board. Ask children what they see
on it. Have them identify the tunnels and chambers.

2. Find the one ant on the game board. Ask what ant they think it
is and why. Accept all answers. Tell them it is the queen ant—
she has a large abdomen and is in a chamber. "What does the
queen ant do?" [lays eggs]

3. Tell the children you are going to put some eggs with the
queen. Have the children help you count five rice grains (eggs)
and place them in the chamber.

4. Ask, "Who helps the queen ant with the eggs and baby ants?"
[nurse ants] Count out and place three nurse ants in the
chamber with the queen and eggs. "How many ants are on the
game board now?" Count four ants.

5. Ask the children what other things they might find in an ant home. As they suggest things, place the appropriate items in the home. For example, if they say a dead grasshopper for food, place a green yarn grasshopper in a chamber. Add other appropriate food to the chambers as they suggest it.

6. Ask what other jobs ants do. If someone suggests that there are guard ants, place two plastic ants near the entrance to the anthill. "Why are there guard ants? What do they do?"

7. Continue placing ants in appropriate places as the children suggest, such as scout ants, nurse ants, housekeeper ants, and baby ants. You may need to ask leading questions to elicit some of the jobs from the children. Keep going until you have placed all the ants mentioned in the previous activities.

8. Once the hill is filled, count all the ants.

9. Tell the children they are going to have their own anthill to fill. Establish the ground rule that no one may touch another person's game board without permission—even when it is time to clean up! Have the children go to the tables or desks.

10. As time and interest allow, provide ample time for the children to freely explore the game board with their own ants, eggs, and food.

11. As the children are filling the game boards, circulate and observe. This is a good opportunity to assess their knowledge of ants. You are likely to hear children talking about their anthills with one another as they fill them, and you can ask them questions about their anthills.

12. At the end of the exploration, have students return their ants, eggs, and yarn pieces to the containers and collect the containers. Let the children eat their pieces of cracker or discard them. You will use these filled containers again in the next session.

optional
The children can draw ants, eggs, and food on their own game boards. Their game boards can go home to be used with family members, be displayed on a bulletin board, and used as a springboard to writing an ant story.

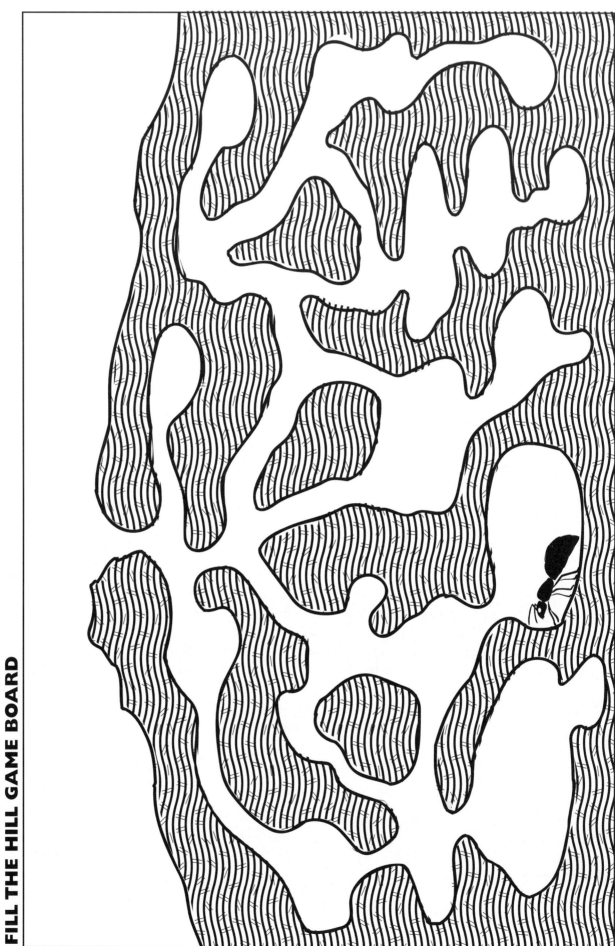

May be duplicated for classroom use.
©1996 by The Regents of the University of California
LHS GEMS—*Ant Homes Under the Ground*

Session 2: Fill the Hill Again!

After the children have independently placed items on their game boards, the whole class listens and fills their anthills according to the directions of their teacher. The children then work with a partner to again place items on their game board. This time each partner has her own game board and they work cooperatively so that the anthills are filled with the same number of ants, eggs, and food items.

What You Need

For each child and yourself
- ❏ 1 Fill the Hill game board
- ❏ 8½" x 11" card stock (It is helpful to have two colors.)
- ❏ 1 plastic container filled with plastic ants, yarn, and rice
- ❏ 1 piece of a cracker for each container

optional
- ❏ Anthill Recording Sheet (page 58 and as a perforated sheet in the back of this book)
- ❏ Fill the Hill card sets A and B for each pair of students (pages 59–60 and as perforated sheets in the back of this book)
- ❏ Pencils, markers or crayons

Getting Ready

Anytime Before the Activity

1. If your children have drawn on the game boards in the first session, then you will need to duplicate another copy of the game board for each child in the class.

2. If you have children record how they filled the anthill, duplicate an Anthill Recording Sheet for each child.

3. If you have the children fill the game board using the Fill the Hill card sets A and B, duplicate the sets on card stock. Each pair of students will need the both sets of cards. It is helpful to duplicate each set onto a different color of card stock to easily distinguish the sets. After duplicating, cut the cards out along the dotted lines to create the card sets and secure the sets with a rubber band.

Just Before the Activity

1. Gather the filled containers from Session 1 and add a piece of a cracker to each container.

2. Have the game boards and containers at tables ready for children to use.

3. If you have the children record how they filled the anthill, gather the Anthill Recording Sheets and writing utensils. Place the sheets and writing utensils in a centrally located spot in the classroom.

4. If you present Game #4 (Fill the Hill Using Cards on page 57), each pair of children should have both sets of cards.

Fill Your Anthill

With younger children, you may want to review the items in the container so everyone is sure what each item represents.

1. Gather the children in the group area away from tables and desks. Tell them they are going to once again fill a game board any way they choose, and then they will get to do a special activity with the game boards.

2. Let the children go to their tables and allow at least five minutes for exploration of the game boards and materials. Walk around the room and observe what the students are doing and saying. Ask them to describe their filled anthill to you.

3. After you feel the children have had sufficient time to explore the boards, ask them for information about their filled boards that they can respond to as a group.
   - "Raise your hand if you have food chambers in your anthill."
   - "Put up the number of fingers for how many guard ants are in your ant home."
   - "Raise your hand if you have scout ants on your game board."

4. Tell the children to clear their game boards by placing all items back in their containers. Tell them they will fill their game boards again in a new way. This time you will tell them something about the anthill and they will fill it exactly as you describe it.

5. Ask the students to find the queen ant on their game boards.
   - "Where is she?" [in a chamber]
   - Ask, "What else could be in the chamber with her?" [eggs and nurse ants]
   - When the children suggest eggs, have them place five eggs (or any number appropriate to your children's abilities) in the chamber.
   - Ask, "What else would be in that chamber?" [nurse ants]
   - Place two nurse ants in the chamber with the queen. "How many ants are in the anthill now?" [three—queen and two nurse ants]

6. Tell the children there are four guard ants at the entrance to the anthill. Count out those ants and place them on the board. Ask them, "How many ants are in the anthill now?" Have them count. [seven ants]

7. Ask, "What other things could go into the chambers." [food] Have students put a green yarn grasshopper in one of the chambers. Put graham crackers in another chamber. Send three scouts out to find more food. "How many ants are on the game board now?" Allow time to count. [10 ants]

8. Ask, "What ants help to keep the home clean?" [housekeeper ants] Put two housekeeper ants in a chamber with cracker crumbs and have them drag out some of the "rotten, old moldy" crumbs.

9. Ask for any observations about the anthill. Count all the ants. "Are there any other jobs ants do?" Place ants according to the suggestions.

10. When you have explored all the suggestions and used all the items you have in the container, choose from the following games.

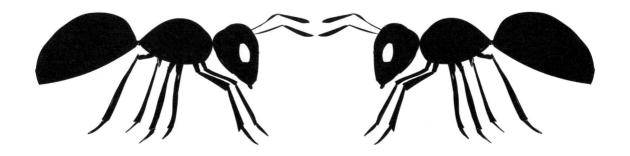

It is very helpful for you to demonstrate these activities before the children do them with their partners.

More Anthill Games

The games are listed from easiest to challenging.

1. Fill the Hill Independently

For preschool children, this is the most appropriate game. Let them fill their game boards as they choose.

2. Copy a Partner

Each child works with a partner. Partner 1 begins by telling Partner 2 where to place an item on the game board as she places the item on her own board. Partner 2 copies her directions and placement on his board. Partner 1 tells the next item to place on the game board. Partner 2 copies. This continues until Partner 1 has placed all the items in the container or until she wants to stop. The partners then switch roles. Partner 2 gives directions and Partner 1 follows.

3. Taking Turns with a Partner

Working with a partner, two children take turns giving directions on how to fill the game board. For example, Partner 1 will begin and say, "Put two guard ants at the entrance." The two children will each put two ants on their game boards. Partner 2 then has a turn to say what goes on the game board next. The partners continue alternating turns until all items are placed on their game boards.

4. Fill the Hill Using Cards

This game is similar to Taking Turns with a Partner, except this time the pairs take turns selecting a card from Set A and both follow the directions to fill their anthills. Children can continue the game with cards from Set B. These cards have both pictures and words, and work well in a free-choice area.

5. Hidden Hill!

CHALLENGING!
Suggested for First Grade—
only after they have done at least one of the other games.

Children work with a partner. Partner 1 puts his game board behind a screen (for example, a file folder or open book) and fills it with a few of the items in the container. Next, Partner 1 gives Partner 2 directions on how to fill her game board just as he has filled his behind the screen. Partner 1 watches as his partner places items on her board. The goal is to have both anthills look alike. He can give as many directions as possible to help his partner. Partner 2 does not get to ask questions! If you try it with your students, you may want to limit the number of items that the partners use—such as 10 ants, four eggs, one grasshopper, two caterpillars, and one cracker crumb.

To ensure success with Game #5, it is recommended you demonstrate how to play. Give each child his own game board, and a cup of ants, caterpillars, grasshoppers, rice, and crackers. Place a file folder in front of you and your board and fill your anthill with a few of the items. Give several directions for the group to follow to make sure all the children are successful in the placement of their items.

Anthill Recording Sheet

If you want your children to use the Anthill Recording Sheet with the various games, demonstrate how to record the contents of the game board using an anthill that has been filled.

    a. Have the students "read" the sheet with you. (You may want to enlarge a copy of the sheet so all the children can see it well.)

    b. As a group, count the number of guard ants. Show them where they would record this number on the sheet. (Record it on your recording sheet.)

    c. Count the scout ants and talk about how to record that number. (Record it on your recording sheet.)

    d. Ask, "How many eggs in this anthill?" "Where would you record it on the sheet?" (Record it on your recording sheet.)

    e. Continue until your sheet is fully recorded and they are familiar with how to complete it.

Have the children fill out their recording sheets after they complete their game(s).

I filled the hill with

_____ **eggs**

_____ **guard ants**

_____ **scout ants**

_____ **nurse ants**

_____ **housekeeper ants**

_____ **crackers**

_____ **caterpillars**

_____ **grasshoppers**

by _____

ANTHILL RECORDING SHEET

May be duplicated for classroom use.
©1996 by The Regents of the University of California
LHS GEMS—_Ant Homes Under the Ground_

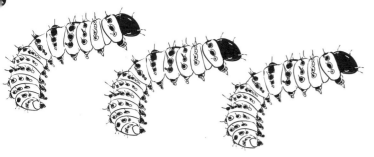

3 caterpillars

Ⓐ

3 guard ants

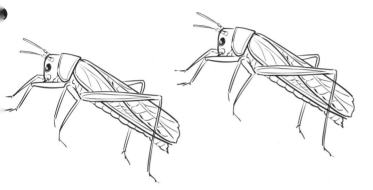

2 grasshoppers

Ⓐ

2 scout ants

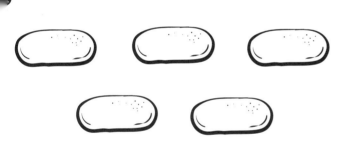

5 eggs

Ⓐ

5 nurse ants

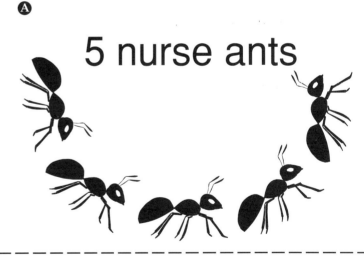

2 crackers

Ⓐ

4 housekeeper ants

May be duplicated for classroom use.
©1996 by The Regents of the University of California
LHS GEMS—*Ant Homes Under the Ground*

B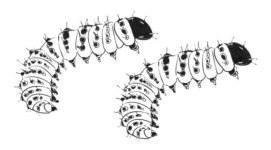

2 caterpillars

B

2 guard ants

B

1 grasshopper

B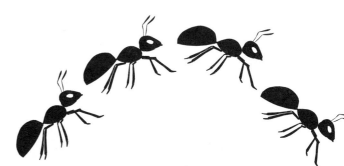

4 scout ants

B

3 eggs

B

3 nurse ants

B

1 cracker

B

2 housekeeper ants

60 May be duplicated for classroom use.
©1996 by The Regents of the University of California
LHS GEMS—*Ant Homes Under the Ground*

Session 3: Fill the Hill Cooperative Game

For Kindergarten and First Grade

After the children play the various games several times both independently and with a partner, they can fill an anthill together according to the directions on special cards.

There are five sets of cards with information on how to fill the anthill. In each set there are four cards. This time, each pair of students shares one game board and one set of materials. Using one set of cards at a time, the pair works together to Fill the Hill.

What You Need

For the whole group
- ❑ 8½" x 11" card stock (It is helpful to have five colors.)
- ❑ Envelopes (large enough to hold the card sets)

For each pair of children and yourself
- ❑ 1 Fill the Hill game board
- ❑ 1 plastic container filled with ants, yarn, and uncooked rice
- ❑ 1 piece of a cracker for each container
- ❑ Fill the Hill card sets 1-5 (pages 64–73 and as perforated sheets in the back of this unit)

optional
- ❑ Anthill Recording Sheet
- ❑ Pencil, marker, or crayon

Getting Ready

Anytime Before the Activity

1. For each pair of children, duplicate and cut out all five Fill the Hill sets of game cards. It is helpful to duplicate each set onto a different colored card stock.

2 Place each set in a different envelope and label it by set.

3. If you have children record how they filled the anthill, duplicate an Anthill Recording Sheet for each pair of children.

Just Before the Activity

1. Gather the filled containers from Sessions 1 and 2 and add a piece of a cracker to each container.

Many teachers said it was very helpful to introduce the vocabulary on the cards to their children before demonstrating how to play these games. Words written on cards then placed in a pocket chart or written on chart paper or a chalkboard were particularly beneficial.

2. Have the game boards, containers, and a set of Fill the Hill #1 cards at tables ready for the children to use.

3. Decide if you will have the additional sets of cards at a central spot in the room, or if you will be the custodian of the cards.

4. If you are going to have the children record on the Anthill Recording Sheet, place it and pencils or markers in a centrally located spot in the classroom.

Fill the Hill Cooperative Game

1. Gather the children in your group area. Hold up a game board and ask them about the different ways they have used it.

2. Tell the children they are going to play a new game. Instead of both partners getting their own game boards and containers of materials, this time two partners will share one board and one container of materials. The partners have four cards to tell them how to fill the anthill. Each partner gets two cards in this game. Show the children a sample of the cards. Hold one up and read it with the children.

3. Demonstrate how to play the game. Choose a child to be your partner. Place one game board and the container of materials between you and the child. Give your partner two cards and take two cards for yourself from Fill the Hill Card Set #1. Read one of your cards aloud. "3 scout ants." Follow the directions and put three scout ants on the game board.

4. Point out where the scout ants are on the cards. Ask, "Where else can scout ants be found?" Let the children know they can place scout ants in any appropriate location on the board. They do not have to copy the placement on the card. This is true for all the cards.

5. Next, have your partner read one of her cards. "4 eggs." She follows the directions on that card and adds the eggs to the game board. Continue with your other card. Read it and place the appropriate items on the game board. Your partner then reads her second card and follows the directions on it.

6. Reread the cards to be sure you and your partner have filled the hill according to the directions. You can trade cards to check. Be sure the children are clear on the steps to follow when they "Fill the Hill."

7. Have the partners go to tables or desks. The tables can be set up with one game board, a container, and a set of cards per pair of children; or the partners can gather game boards, containers of materials, and a set of cards before they go to their tables.

8. If you have the children use the Anthill Recording Sheet, remind them to fill out the sheets after each game.

9. After the children have completed a game with one set of cards, they can continue with another set of cards. Either the pairs of children can trade the set they complete with a new set from you, or they can return the set they have completed and take another set from a central location. Be sure they only have one set at a time!

Going Further

1. Children can fill their anthill and generate number stories about the things in their anthill.
   - "My anthill has 2 guard ants and 3 nurse ants, which makes 5 ants altogether."
   - "My anthill has 1 queen ant and 5 eggs, which is 6 items in 1 chamber."

2. The children can be told there are six ants in the anthill, and asked to tell a story about those ants.
   - " I have 2 guard ants and 2 nurse ants and 2 housekeeper ants."
   - " I have 4 scout ants and 2 guard ants."

3. Read the book *One Hundred Hungry Ants* (See Literature Connections on page 84). In the book, 100 ants march in different arrangements, which introduces the children to this large number in concrete terms. You may want to have your children use 12 ants to march in the following ways: by 2's, by 3's, and by 4's.

4. With a filled game board, reverse the game and have the children practice subtraction by using the cards to take ants, food, and eggs off their game board.

5. Give pairs of students a set of four blank cards. Have them create their own set of Fill the Hill cards.

Fill the Hill #1

3 scout ants

Fill the Hill #1

1 grasshopper and 1 ant

May be duplicated for classroom use.
©1996 by The Regents of the University of California
LHS GEMS—*Ant Homes Under the Ground*

Fill the Hill #1

2 guard ants

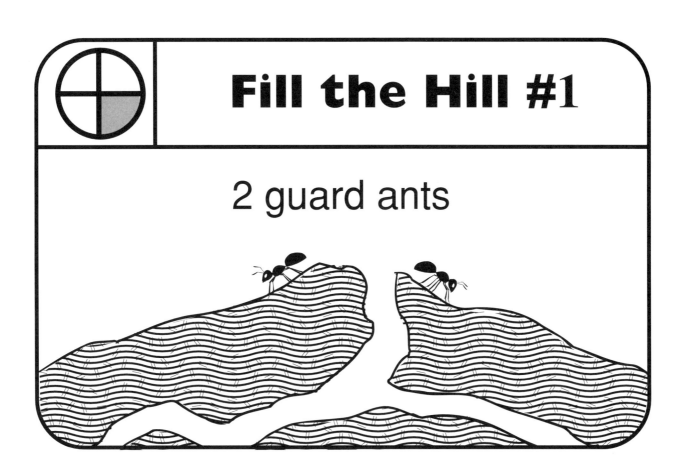

Fill the Hill #1

4 eggs

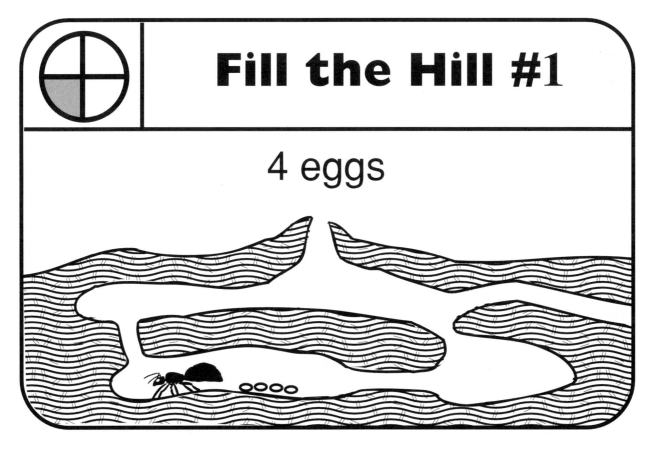

May be duplicated for classroom use.
©1996 by The Regents of the University of California
LHS GEMS—*Ant Homes Under the Ground*

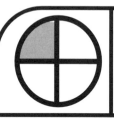

Fill the Hill #2

2 guard ants

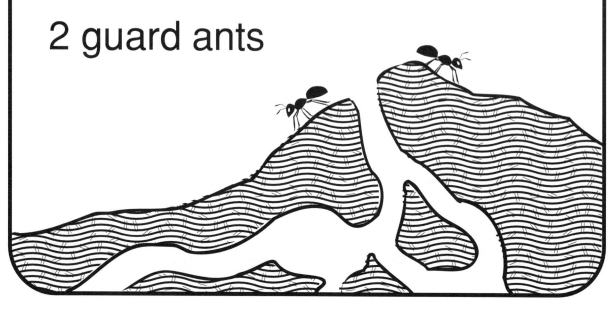

Fill the Hill #2

5 scout ants

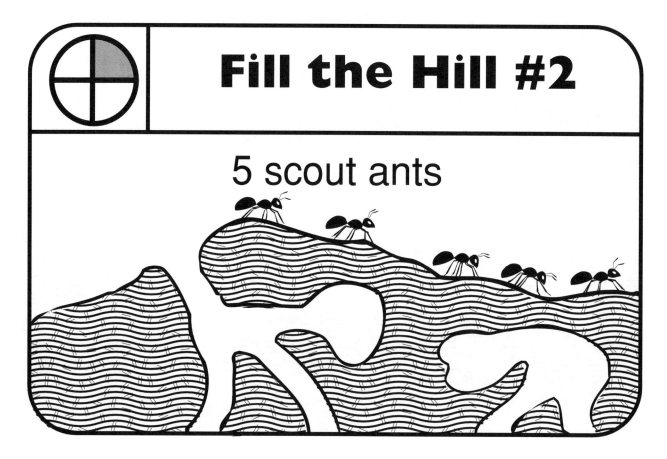

May be duplicated for classroom use.
©1996 by The Regents of the University of California
LHS GEMS—*Ant Homes Under the Ground*

Fill the Hill #2

1 caterpillar and 2 ants

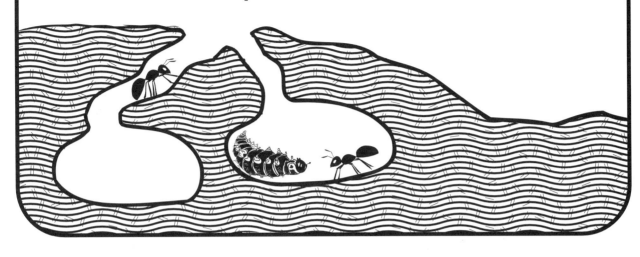

Fill the Hill #2

6 eggs

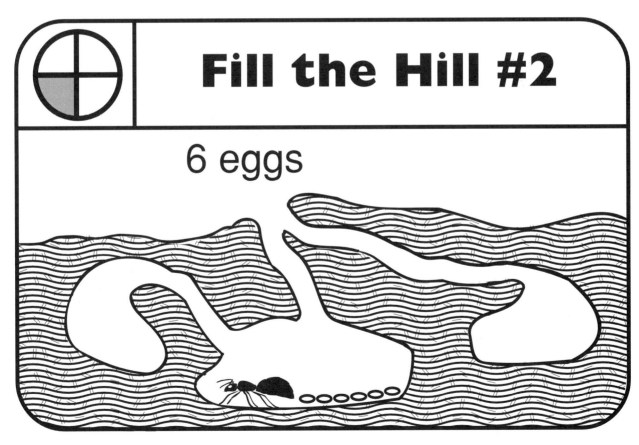

May be duplicated for classroom use.
©1996 by The Regents of the University of California
LHS GEMS—*Ant Homes Under the Ground*

Fill the Hill #3

2 caterpillars and 3 ants

Fill the Hill #3

3 guard ants

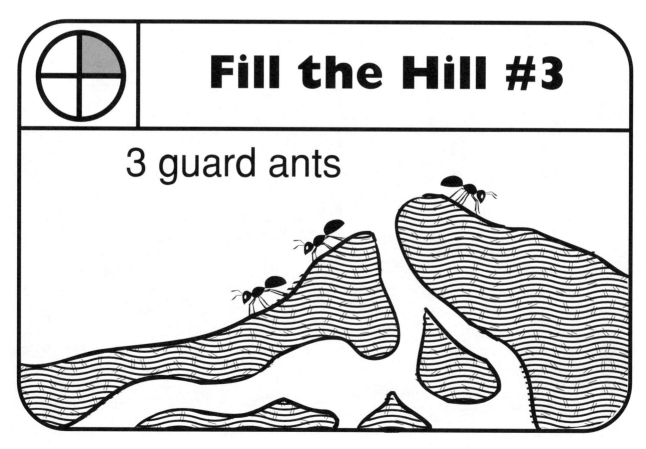

May be duplicated for classroom use.
©1996 by The Regents of the University of California
LHS GEMS—*Ant Homes Under the Ground*

Fill the Hill #3

2 grasshoppers

Fill the Hill #3

6 scout ants

May be duplicated for classroom use.
©1996 by The Regents of the University of California
LHS GEMS—*Ant Homes Under the Ground*

Fill the Hill #4

2 housekeeper ants

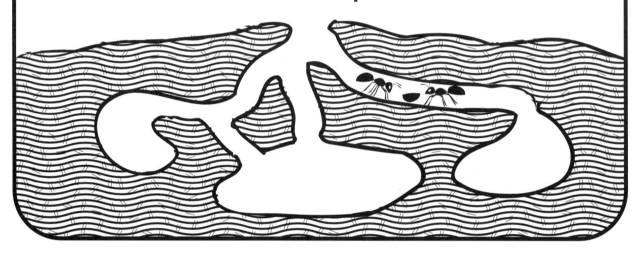

Fill the Hill #4

4 scout ants

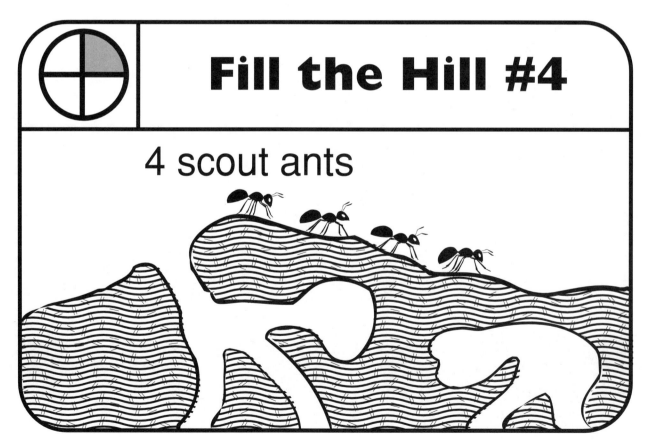

May be duplicated for classroom use.

Fill the Hill #4

2 grasshoppers

Fill the Hill #4

5 nurse ants and 3 eggs

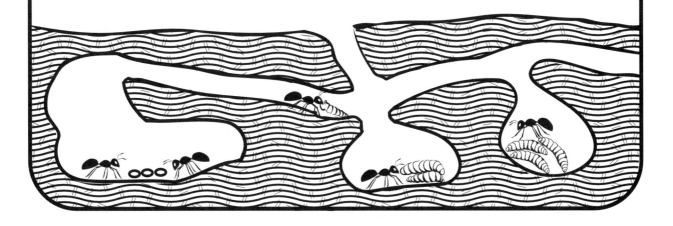

May be duplicated for classroom use.
©1996 by The Regents of the University of California
LHS GEMS—*Ant Homes Under the Ground*

Fill the Hill #5

3 caterpillars and 6 ants

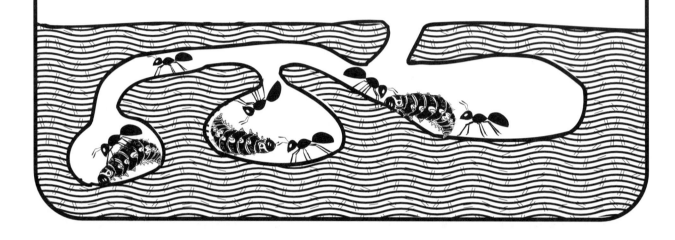

Fill the Hill #5

4 guard ants

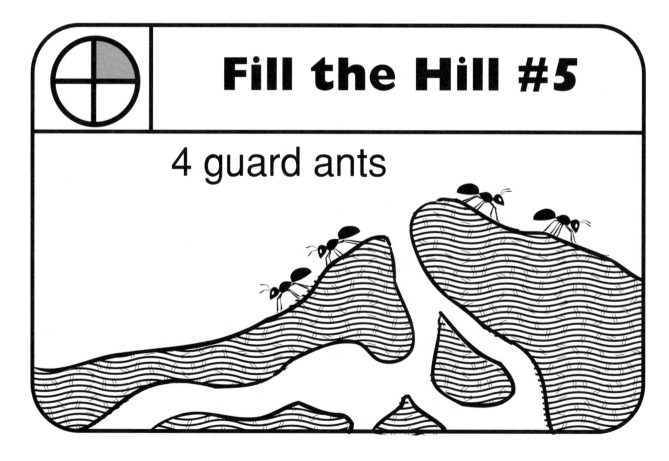

May be duplicated for classroom use.
©1996 by The Regents of the University of California
LHS GEMS—*Ant Homes Under the Ground*

Fill the Hill #5

8 eggs with the queen ant

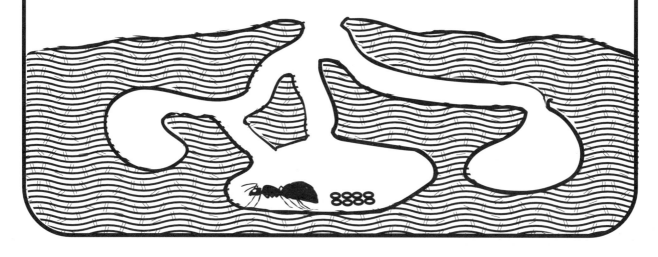

Fill the Hill #5

6 nurse ants

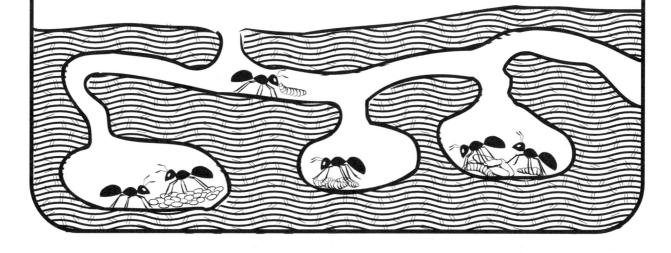

May be duplicated for classroom use.
©1996 by The Regents of the University of California
LHS GEMS—*Ant Homes Under the Ground*

Background Information

This background section is for your information and use, and is not meant to be read out loud to your students. The information is presented to help you answer many of the questions enthusiastic children, parents, and other teachers will ask. It may also give you ideas for extending activities and developing new ones.

Variety of Ants

At any one time, it is estimated that at least 1 quadrillion ants are alive on earth. There are at least 10,000 different kinds of ants, and these insects, which are related to bees and wasps, have been around for more than 100 million years.

While the homes of ants are often diverse, most live in nests in the ground, wood, or in natural cavities. However, some notable exceptions include the weaver ants of Africa, Asia, and Australia that live in trees and weave leaves to make nests. The army ants of South America and the driver ants of Africa have no permanent nests. On the move most of the time, these ants carry their young with them as they search the countryside for food.

The feeding behaviors of ants also vary greatly. The leaf-cutter ants of South America cut leaves to use as compost for growing a special kind of fungus, which they eat. The harvester ants collect and store grain for food. The honey pot ants use their bodies to store nectar, which nourishes the ant community when food is scarce.

The common, brown garden ant is featured in *Ant Homes Under the Ground.* This ant eats scraps of food from our houses as well as dead insects, juice from aphids, and nectar from flowers. It digs tunnels and chambers in the earth to build its home. The ant piles the dirt, which it removes from its tunnels, in a neat mound at the entrance. Other mound builders are the harvester ants, small yellow meadow ants, and wood ants.

Body Structure of Queen, Male, and Worker Ants

Ants, like other insects, have bodies that are divided into three main parts: a head, a thorax, and an abdomen. Ants have six legs, two antennae, and two compound eyes. Some ants also have three simple eyes, called *ocelli*, which are sensitive to light and dark. Ants have two claws on each foot, which they use to dig, climb, and fight. Male ants and young queens have four wings. The two antennae on the front of the ant's head are slender, jointed appendages used for smelling and touching, and possibly for hearing. The antennae are vital to an ant since its sense of smell helps it find food, recognize danger, and identify other members of its colony.

Ants also have a special stomach called a *crop*. When worker ants collect food, they carry it back to the nest in their crop. They regurgitate the food to feed other members of the colony. They can store food in their crops for long periods of time to distribute when needed.

Ant Sizes

Different species of ants range in size from the small brown garden ant to the 1½-inch-long bulldog ant of Australia. Queens, males, and workers within a species are different sizes. The queens are the largest ants in a colony, and the workers are the smallest. Sometimes the size of the workers in a colony will vary depending on the job the worker does. The smaller worker has jobs such as cleaning and feeding other ants, whereas the larger worker has more aggressive roles such as guarding the anthill.

Ant Life Span

The queen ant lives considerably longer than the female worker or the male. A queen may live 20 years or more. One brown garden ant queen lived 29 years in captivity. A worker may live as many as seven years, and a male typically dies shortly after its mating flight. An anthill may outlast a human lifetime.

Ant Strength

Ants can lift and carry 10 to 50 times their own weight. If an average adult human were as strong as an ant, she could lift a car.

Ant Society

All ants are social, living in colonies with one or more queens, female workers, winged males, and winged young queens. The colonies often contain upwards of 20 million individuals, and almost all are female. The males and young queens need wings for their nuptial flight, during which the males fertilize the young queens. A queen ant only needs to be fertilized once in her lifetime. Once fertilized, a young queen loses her wings and begins her lifelong job of laying eggs. Since a male ant's only job is fertilization, he dies soon after mating. Female workers do a variety of jobs. The brown garden ant workers dig tunnels and chambers to build a nest, clean and repair the nest, care for the queens and young, and defend the anthill. They also leave the nest to collect food to share with all the members of the ant community.

Metamorphosis

When a queen ant mates, she stores millions of live sperm cells in a pouch in her abdomen. After mating, the queen begins laying eggs. Some worker ants feed and clean the queen. Others, commonly called nurse ants, take the eggs from the queen and put them in nurseries. The eggs hatch into white, wormlike creatures called *larvae.*

The nurse ants feed the larvae and, using their saliva, clean the eggs and larvae. The saliva makes the eggs or larvae stick together in clumps, making it easier for the nurse ants to move them when the chambers get too hot, too cold, or too wet.

The food that the workers feed to the larvae depends on the species. Some ants feed regurgitated liquids to their young, harvester ants feed seed parts to their larvae, and army ants feed insect parts to their larvae.

Queen, male, and worker larvae all look alike at first. As they grow, some become much fatter than others. The largest larvae become queens, the middle-size ones become males, and the smallest become female workers.

After about 15 to 30 days, the larvae use silk, secreted from glands near their mouths, to spin cocoons. Some ant larvae species do not build cocoons; their tough skin provides enough protection. Inside their cocoons or skins, the larvae change to pupae. The pupae, over a period of 13–22 days, develop into adult ants. The nurse ants help the young adults, which at first are white and somewhat transparent, emerge from their encasements. This change from egg to adult, called *metamorphosis*, takes about three months.

Scent Trail

An ant becomes excited when it finds food. On its way back to its nest, it dabs the end of its abdomen on the ground, leaving chemical substances called *pheromones.* These chemicals produce a scent. Other ants from the nest follow the scent to the food, leaving more scent on the trail as they carry food back to the nest. When there is no more food left, the ants stop dabbing the pheromones, and the scent trail goes away in a few minutes.

Ant Enemies and Defense

Ants have many enemies, such as birds, frogs, toads, lizards, spiders, anteaters, and other insects, including other ants. Red ants often attack anthills of black ants to steal the cocoons. The black ants that hatch from these cocoons become slaves of the red ants. People kill ants by stepping on them and spraying them with insecticides.

As a defense, ants bite and sting. Some ants spray a chemical from the tips of their abdomens as a warning when they detect danger. Sometimes after biting an enemy, an ant will spray chemicals into the open wound.

Resources

All Upon A Sidewalk
by Jean Craighead George
Dutton, New York, 1974.

An Ant Colony
by Heiderose and Andreas Fischer-Nagel
Carolrhoda Books, Minneapolis, 1989.

Ant
by David Hawcock and Lee Montgomery
Random House, New York, 1994.

The Ant Book
by Luann Colombo
Andrews and McMeel, Kansas City, MO, 1994.

Ant Cities
by Arthur Dorros
Thomas Y. Crowell, New York, 1987.

Ant: Life Story
by Michael Chinery
Troll Associates, Mahwah, N.J., 1991.

Ants
by Angels Julivert
Barron's, Hauppauge, N.Y., 1991.

Ants
by Cynthia Overbeck
Lerner Publications, Minneapolis, 1982.

Ants Are Fun
by Mildred Myrick
Harper & Row, New York, 1968.

Ants: Keeping Minibeasts
by Barrie Watts
Franklin Watts, New York, 1990.

Armies of Ants
by Walter Retan
Scholastic, New York, 1994.

Discovering Ants
by Christopher O'Toole
Bookwright Press, New York, 1986.

Hidden Messages
by Dorothy Van Woerkom
Crown Publishers, New York, 1979.

If You Were An Ant
by Barbara Brenner
Harper & Row, New York, 1973.

If You Were An Ant
by S. J. Calder
Silver Press, Englewood Cliffs, N.J., 1989.

Insects Build Their Homes
by Gladys Conklin
Holiday House, New York, 1972.

The Life Cycle of an Ant
by Trevor Terry and Margaret Linton
Bookwright Press, N.Y., 1988.

Looking At Ants
by Dorothy Hinshaw Patent
Holiday House, New York, 1989.

"Queen of the Hill"
Ranger Rick, vol. 10, no. 13, Dec. 1982.

questions and answers about Ants
by Millicent E. Selsam
Four Winds Press, N.Y., 1967.

Those Amazing Ants
by Patricia Brennan Demuth
Macmillan, New York, 1994.

When Insects Are Babies
by Gladys Conklin
Holiday House, New York, 1969.

Resource Materials

You probably can purchase an ant farm from your local toy or hardware store. You can also mail order ants and ant farms from the addresses below. *Note:* The shipment of ants is not permitted outside the continental limits of the United States

Uncle Milton's
5717 Corsa Avenue
Westlake Village, CA 91362
(818) 707-0800

The Ant House
National Science Industries, Ltd.
51-01 Far Rockaway Beach Blvd.
Far Rockaway, N.Y. 11691

Internet

Myrmecology (the scientific study of ants) is the subject of this World Wide Web page. It has illustrations of various ants and ant nests, facts and figures, as well as how to build your own ant farm.   http://members.aol.com/dinarda/ant/index

Computer Game

SimAnt is a simulation/learning game like SimCity or SimEarth. In SimAnt, a player is the leader of a colony of black ants whose mission is to fight off an invasion of red ants and human influences, then take over a yard and a house. There are maps of underground and above ground habitats. In an experimental mode, a player can insert various objects and see how the SimAnts react. Recommended for ages 8 and up, but you may want to check it out.

Maxis Software
2121 N. California Blvd. Suite 600
Walnut Creek, CA 94596-3572
(800) 336-2947

Literature Connections

You may wish to examine the literature listings for the GEMS teacher's guides Animal Defenses, Buzzing A Hive, Group Solutions, Hide A Butterfly, Ladybugs, Tree Homes, Penguins And Their Young, *and* Terrarium Habitats *in the GEMS handbook* Once Upon A GEMS Guide: Connecting Young People's Literature to Great Explorations in Math and Science. *Also, please see the age-appropriate listings in the science themes as well as the math strands sections in the handbook. In addition, the teacher's guides include exciting activities that would make excellent accompaniments to this guide.*

Aardvark's Picnic
by Jon Atlas Higham
Little, Brown, Boston. 1986
Grades: Preschool–4

When Aardvark plans a picnic for his friends he is sad to discover he can't find the ants needed for some tasty picnic treats. He decides he'll have to find some as he travels to the picnic site. Along the way Aardvark meets other friends with different picnic food ideas, but finds no ants. Young readers will delight in spotting the ants that Aardvark misses. When Aardvark meets his friends at the picnic it is very evident there are plenty of ants. This is one picnic where ants are welcome guests!

Amazing Anthony Ant
by Lorna and Graham Philpot
Random House, New York. 1994
Grades: Preschool–4

In this innovative, hands-on book, you participate in many ways—by singing the text of the story, by lifting one of four flaps to complete the verse, by finding Anthony in an underground maze full of interesting and humorous places, and by following the maze as Anthony followed it. Across the top of each page is the long line of rapidly multiplying small ants, which makes a great visual for understanding multiples. Be forewarned, the biological information about ants is slightly skewed.

Ant and Bee and Kind Dog
by Angela Banner; illustrated by Bryan Ward
Heinemann, London. 1992
Grades: Preschool–2

When Kind Dog smells a good smell, he and Ant and Bee try to track it down. Their adventure occurs alphabetically—to find the smell, Kind Dog sniffs the air; they all walk along and find a bell, a camel, and a duck. Other Ant and Bee books help readers learn colors, shapes, counting, and days of the week.

The Ant and the Elephant
by Bill Peet
Houghton Mifflin, Boston. 1972
Grades: Preschool–4

When a tiny ant becomes stranded in the middle of a river, he seeks the help of a turtle who refuses to inconvenience himself. When the turtle himself needs help he asks a hornbill who says she will not oblige. In a chain of events, each selfish animal refuses to help another until finally several jungle animals find themselves in trouble. An elephant taking a stroll helps not only the ant but the other animals as well. Then, when the elephant needs help, the ant returns the favor—with the help of 95,000 friends. This is a good example of the benefits of cooperation.

Anthony Ant's Creepy Crawly Party
by Lorna and Graham Philpot
Random House, New York. 1995
Grades: Preschool–4

Like *Amazing Anthony Ant* by the same authors, this is a hands-on, reader-participation book. Readers follow Anthony through an underground maze as he delivers party invitations then look for his friends under a pair of flaps. The final page shows Anthony's party in full swing with a caterpillar cake with aphid milk for the guests. In looking for Anthony's insect friends in their underground homes, readers develop their visual discrimination skills, and in following the mazes, mathematics skills are developed.

Ants Don't Get Sunday Off
by Penny Pollock; illustrated by Lorinda Bryan Cauley
Putnam, New York. 1978
Grades: K–3

Anya, a busy and tired worker ant, longs for a little break from her chores. Nevertheless, when heavy rains threaten her nest, she takes charge and leads the workers as they rescue the queen and young ants. However, Anya becomes separated. When she tries to find the nest, Anya has many adventures. This easy-reader book includes a nice map of Anya's underground home as well as a map tracking her adventure. Facts about young ants, ant tunnels, and jobs of worker ants are nicely folded into the story.

Babushka's Doll
by Patricia Polacco
Simon & Schuster, New York. 1990
Grades: K–3

Natasha is a demanding and rambunctious little girl who
borrows a doll that turns out to be even more demanding than
she is. Natasha learns something about herself—and that
playing with Babushka's doll once is enough! A good book to
start a discussion about cooperative behavior.

Flit, Flutter, Fly!
Poems About Bugs and Other Crawly Creatures
selected by Lee Bennett Hopkins; illustrated by Peter Palagonia
Doubleday, New York. 1992
Grades: Preschool–2

This collection of poems by a variety of authors is about insects
and other creatures that crawl, including a delightful poem
about ants. Reading these simple poems fosters an appreciation
for small creatures. The poems are gentle and the illustrations
are soothing—a perfect combination for young children.

"I Can't" Said the Ant: A Second Book of Nonsense
by Polly Cameron
Coward, McCann & Geoghegan, New York. 1961
Grades: K–3

When a teapot falls off the drain board, the whole kitchen asks a
passing ant to rescue her. Unable to perform the task alone, the
ant recruits the help of many other ants and two spiders—and
they cooperatively rescue the teapot. This easy-reader book has
a playful rhyming text.

In the Tall, Tall Grass
by Denise Fleming
Henry Holt, New York. 1991
Grades: Preschool–K

The rhymed text tells of the many creatures to be found in a
grassy area. As viewed by a caterpillar moving through the tall
grass, the colorful illustrations show a variety of creatures—
from beetles to bats—each doing something different in the
grass.

It's Mine!
by Leo Lionni
Alfred A. Knopf, New York. 1985
Grades: Preschool–2

Three quarrelsome frogs quibble over the ownership of a pond, an island, and even the air! A storm makes them value the benefits of sharing when they must share the last rock remaining above a flood. This story is a good way to introduce the merits of cooperation before beginning cooperative activities.

John J. Plenty and Fiddler Dan:
A New Fable of the Grasshopper and the Ant
by John Ciardi; illustrated by Madeleine Gekiere
Lippincott, Philadelphia. 1963
Grades: K–6

Aesop's classic tale of the Grasshopper and the Ant is retold in poetic verse and has some surprising twists. This is a good connection with Activity 3, Sessions 2 and 3, since it deals with food storage.

The Little Red Ant and the Great Big Crumb
by Shirley Climo; illustrated by Francisco X. Mora
Clarion Books, New York. 1995
Grades: K–4

In this retelling of a Mexican fable, a small red ant feels unable to carry the large crumb of food she finds in a cornfield. She seeks the help of many others, but finally realizes she is the strongest among them. Many Spanish words and phrases are used in a natural way throughout the story and are defined in the back of the book. The moral: You can if you think you can.

The Magic School Bus Gets Ants in its Pants:
A Book About Ants
by Linda Ward Beech and illustrated by John Speirs
Scholastic, New York. 1996
Grades: 1–5

As the class project for the science fair, Ms. Frizzle's class makes a movie about ants. In the style that has made the Magic School Bus so popular, the class really "gets into" their project—they shrink and go into an anthill. The different jobs ants perform, ant communication, food sharing, tunnel structure, and life stages are clearly explained. With Ms. Frizzle's help, the class realizes that the ants work together cooperatively, and that every ant's job is important for the survival of all. As in other Magic School Bus books, there is a page of facts in the back of the book, plus an anthill project for parents and children.

Night Visitors
by Ed Young
Philomel Books, New York. 1995
Grades: 1–6

When ants invade his family's rice storehouse, young Ho Kuan, who has great respect for all forms of life, must find a way to seal the storehouse to keep the ants out before his father kills them all. In what may or may not be a dream, he becomes part of an ant colony and finds a solution. In this retelling of a Chinese folk tale, many aspects of ant behavior and society are shown.

One Hundred Hungry Ants
by Elinor J. Pinczes; illustrated by Bonnie MacKain
Houghton Mifflin, Boston. 1993
Grades: Preschool–3

As an ant colony swarms toward a picnic, the tiniest ant stops the march and suggests they divide into different line formations to arrive at the picnic quicker. In all the divisions of one hundred, the illustrations show the correct number of ants in each line. In the end, however, the rearrangements cause the ants to miss out on all the food. This is a great math connection to division and making change for a dollar. Told in lilting rhyme, this playful story is suggested as a Going Further for Activity 5, Session 3.

A Remainder of One
by Elinor J. Pinczes; illustrated by Bonnie MacKain
Houghton Mifflin, Boston. 1995
Grades: Preschool–3

When the 25th squadron of bugs, including ants, march past their queen, she is dismayed to see that the lines are uneven. One bug, Joe by name, is left behind—a remainder of one. Knowing that their queen does not like untidy lines, the bugs divide themselves into different lines. It is only after several tries that Joe is included in even lines that march by the queen to the delight of all. Colorful and playful illustrations make this a math connection that introduces the concept of division and remainders and makes a good connection to the Going Further in Activity 5, Session 3.

Step by Step
by Diane Wolkstein; illustrated by Jos. A. Smith
Morrow Junior Books, New York. 1994
Grades: Preschool–1

A little ant and her friend want to spend a day together. To reach her friend, the ant travels carefully, step by step over stones, across a leaf, and under a branch. Students may notice that the little ant has only four shoes even though ants have six legs. The watercolor illustrations do a great job of showing the world from the small ant's perspective.

There's an Ant in Anthony
by Bernard Most
Morrow, New York. 1980
Grades: Preschool–3

After discovering an "ant" in his own name at school one day, Anthony searches for an "ant" in a variety of words and places. Each time Anthony finds an ant in a word, he picks it up and puts it in a jar. Readers can follow along counting the number of ants Anthony has in his jar—and the number of ants that find Anthony's pants when he rests in a park!

Two Bad Ants
by Chris Van Allsburg
Houghton Mifflin, Boston. 1988
Grades: Preschool–4

When a colony of ants sets off in search of sugar to feed their queen, it becomes a dangerous adventure for two curious ants who stay behind. Ants are portrayed as social creatures who live best when they work together for a common goal. The illustrations, from the ant's perspective, make a strong connection to scale. You could ask, "How was the scout able to find her way back to the sugar?" as a good connection to Activity 3, Session 1.

Assessment Suggestions

Selected Student Outcomes

1. Students become familiar with ant body structure and behavior as they observe and care for live ants.

2. Students create models of ants and an underground nest, and use them to enact ant behaviors through cooperative play.

3. Students become familiar with the different life stages of the ant.

4. Students are able to describe the various jobs ants perform during their adult life.

5. Students develop number, spatial reasoning, and cooperative work skills as they solve problems together.

Built-in Assessment Activities

Live Ants Outdoors and Indoors

In Activity 1: Ants, Ants, Ants, students observe live ants outdoors and maintain a living ant farm. They study ant body structure, as well as feeding, and tunneling behaviors. Through questions and discussions, the teacher notes how students describe and compare their observations of ants.
(Outcomes 1, 4)

Anthills on the Wall

In Activity 2: Ants and Ant Tunnels, students create their own paper models of ants based on their observations of live ants. After role-playing tunneling, and observing the Ant Nest poster, students cooperatively build an anthill mural. By asking students to discuss their ant model and anthill mural, the teacher uses their responses and model projects to assess their understanding.
(Outcomes 1, 2, 4)

Scout Ants

In Activity 3, Session 1: Scouts and Guards, students participate in a drama and role play that introduces how scout ants find and collect food for the ant community. Students pretend they are ants and follow a scent trail to the food. During these activities, the teacher listens for descriptive language, explanations, responses, and questions about this particular ant job.
(Outcomes 1, 4)

Egg, Larvae, Pupae, Adult

In Activity 4: How Ants Grow and Change, students discover the life stages of the ant. New sections of the Ant nest poster are overlaid on the old poster and it is displayed on a classroom wall. Students are asked to find what is different in these drawings. As they discover the queen, eggs, larvae and pupae, the teacher asks questions and guides a discussion about the ant's life cycle. The poster remains up for students to informally observe. The teacher can note responses and questions about the ant life cycle and observe whether students use the new vocabulary and concepts in other play and discussion situations.
(Outcomes 3, 4)

What's in Our Anthill?

In Activity 5: Fill the Hill, students play a cooperative math game that challenges them to fill an anthill game board with plastic ants, eggs, and food items according to the directions on various sets of cards. At the end of the games, the students check to see if they have followed the directions correctly, and then record the numbers of each item on a data sheet. The teacher can observe each student's progress during the game and can use the data sheets as feedback.
(Outcome 5)

Additional Assessment Ideas

Stories and Plays

Students can write and dictate stories or create an Ant Book about indoor and outdoor ants they have observed. Stories can become a classroom play performed for families or other classes.
(Outcomes 1, 2, 3, 4)

Ants at Home

Challenge families to find and observe ant trails at home. Ask students to keep a journal of an ant trail for one week and share it with the class.
(Outcomes 1, 3, 4)

What Do You See?

Ask students to observe the Ant Nest poster and describe the various relationships between the ants, food, and chambers. Students could observe just one section of the poster and write or dictate a story based on what they see.
(Outcomes 3, 4, 5)

Fill the Hill My Way

Have students design and illustrate their own sets of cards for the Fill the Hill games and challenge fellow students.
(Outcomes 3, 4, 5)

Summary Outlines

Activity 1: Ants, Ants, Ants

Session 1: The Ant Hunt

1. Show a mound of dirt.
   Ask, "What animal do you think could crawl through this tiny hole to its underground home?"
2. Ask, "Where have you seen ants?"
   "What were they doing?"
3. Take the children for a walk to look for ants.
4. Have the children leave food for ants. Dampen the ground and put a board or stone on the ground in hope ants will make a nest underneath. Tell the children they will return regularly to dampen the soil and observe.
5. Let the children talk about what they found.

Session 2: The Ant Farm

1. Set up an Ant Farm with children. Let them take turns using eye droppers to dampen the sand. Feed the ants.
2. Leave the Ant Farm where children can watch the ants dig tunnels and chambers. Caution the students not to move the ant farm.
3. Set up an ant farm feeding and watering schedule.

Activity 2: Ants and Ant Tunnels

Session 1: A Closer Look at Ants
Looking at the Ant Poster

Show the Ant poster. Have the children count the ant's body parts.

Making a Paper Ant

The children help you make a paper ant and then they make their own either from precut pieces or from their own design.

Session 2: Ant Tunnels
The Ant Farm

Children observe tunnels and tell what they saw ants doing.

Tunnels

1. Show sections 1 and 2 of the Ant nest poster. Ask, "What do you think the ants are doing?" Tell the children ants use the

tunnels and rooms like the children use hallways and rooms in their own homes. If appropriate, tell class that the rooms are called *chambers*.

2. Compare ways people and ants dig tunnels.
3. Children role-play ants crawling through tunnels and in and out of chambers.
4. Leave the ant books out for the students to look at.
5. Hang the poster in room where the children can see it.

For First Grade

1. Have a child use a finger to trace the tunnels in the ant farm.
2. Introduce the Ant Farm Activity Sheet and give a sheet to each child.
3. Let the students draw ants and tunnels on their sheets.

Session 3: The Ant Nest Mural

The Ant Nest Mural Drama

1. In a circle, present a short tunneling drama using the large mural.
2. Give each child one tunnel and one chamber to place on the mural to continue drama and to give an idea of what the finished mural may look like.
3. After the drama, pick up paper ants, tunnels, and chambers.

Beginning the Mural

1. Each child glues one paper chamber and two tunnels on small sheet of paper.
2. The children arrange their pictures on large mural, trying to make the tunnels connect.
3. Let the children place their paper ants on the mural.
4. Tell the children they will leave their ants and ant homes at school because they will make more things to add to the mural.

Activity 3: What Happens Inside an Ant's Home?

Session 1: Scouts and Guards

The Scout Ants Drama

1. Present a drama with paper ants dabbing the ends of their abdomen to leave a scent trail.
2. Introduce scout ants.
3. Ask a few questions to review concepts introduced in drama.

Following the Scent Trail

Using scented cotton balls, the children role-play ants leaving a scent trail and carrying food back to the nest.

Guarding the Nest

The children role play guard ants protecting the nest from ants with a different scent.

Session 2: Dragging Food into the Nest

The children role-play ants dragging a caterpillar or bug through a tunnel.

Session 3: More Ant Food

The Ant Walk

Check food left outside to see what the ants ate.

The Ant Farm

Have a child drop food into the Ant Farm.

The Ant Food Poster

1. The children observe the assembled Ant Nest poster. Ask, "What are the ants doing now?"
2. Have a child find a chamber with a grasshopper.
3. Have a child find scout ants. Have another child find guard ants.
4. Introduce housekeeper ants.

For First Grade

Write the words scout ants, guard ants, and housekeeper ants to familiarize your students with them.

Activity 4: How Ants Grow and Change

The Ant Farm

Encourage the students to check the Ant Farm.

For First Grade

Let the students draw new Ant Farm Activity Sheets and compare them with the previous sheets.

The Queen Ant

1. The children observe the Ant Nest poster with section 5 overlaid. Ask, "Do you see anything new that the ants are doing in their nest?" [queen laying eggs, ants carrying eggs]
2. Introduce nurse ants.
3. Ask, "What do you think the baby ants will look like when they hatch out of the eggs?" Tell the children newly hatched baby ants are white and look like tiny worms.
4. Show pictures of ant eggs and larvae. Leave the pictures out for the children to look at later.
5. Leave the poster on the wall until you finish all the ant activities.

For First Grade

1. The children observe the Ant Nest poster with section 6 overlaid. Ask, "What do you think is happening in this picture?"
2. Have a child point to the chamber with the baby ants. If appropriate, introduce the word *larvae.*
3. Have a child point to a nurse ant that is carrying a baby ant to a warmer chamber.
4. Tell the group that baby ants, like caterpillars, spin cocoons. Have a child point to a cocoon. Tell the children that inside the cocoon baby ants stay very still and slowly turn into grown-up ants. If appropriate, introduce the word *pupae.*
5. Ask a child to point to a white ant that has just hatched from a cocoon.
6. Review life cycle on poster by having a child point to egg, larva, pupa, adult.
7. Role play with the children the four stages of egg, larva, pupa, and adult ant.

The Ant Mural Grows

1. Place one new chamber and tunnel on the floor and walk one child's ant and the queen ant onto the chamber. Ask, "Which ant do you think is the queen?" "Why do you think she is so big?" [full of eggs]
2. Pretend queen is laying eggs and draw eggs in chamber.
3. Tape the queen in the chamber and attach the new chamber and tunnel to the mural.
4. The children decide what jobs they want their ants to do, and they add something new to the mural.
5. When the children finish with the mural, let them take their ants, chambers, and tunnels home.

For Kindergarten and First Grade

Write the words larvae and pupae so the students begin to recognize the words.

Activity 5: Fill the Hill

Session 1: Introducing the Ant Home Game Board

1. Hold up game board and ask children what they see on it. Identify the tunnels and chambers.
2. Identify queen and ask what job she does. Put eggs on board. Have the children count them with you.
3. Ask the children what else might they find in anthill. As they suggest things, place the appropriate items on the game board. Have the children count the items with you.
4. Give each child a game board and ant materials to play with.

Session 2: Fill Your Ant Home

1. Let the children play freely with the game board.
2. Ask for information about their filled boards such as: "Raise your hand if you have scout ants on your game board." "Put up the number of fingers to show how many nurse ants you have in your ant home."
3. Have the children clear their boards.
4. Using the cards, tell the children how many ants, eggs, and food to place on their game board.
5. As the children fill the board, ask for totals. "How many ants are in the ant home now?"
6. The children take partners and fill the game boards using the cards.

Session 3: Fill the Hill Cooperative Game
For Kindergarten and First Grade

1. Demonstrate how to play the game. Choose a child to be your partner. Share one game board and one container of materials. Each of you has two cards of one set. Read one card and you follow the directions. Have the child read a card and she follows the directions. Repeat with the remaining cards.
2. Have the children pair up and play the game.
3. When the children have finished with a set of cards, they can get another set and play again. Make sure each pair of students has only one set at a time.

I filled the hill with

_____ eggs

_____ guard ants

_____ scout ants

_____ nurse ants

_____ housekeeper ants

_____ crackers

_____ caterpillars

_____ grasshoppers

by _____

ANTHILL RECORDING SHEET

May be duplicated for classroom use.
©1996 by The Regents of the University of California
LHS GEMS—*Ant Homes Under the Ground*

PATTERN D
(Queen Ant Body and Head)

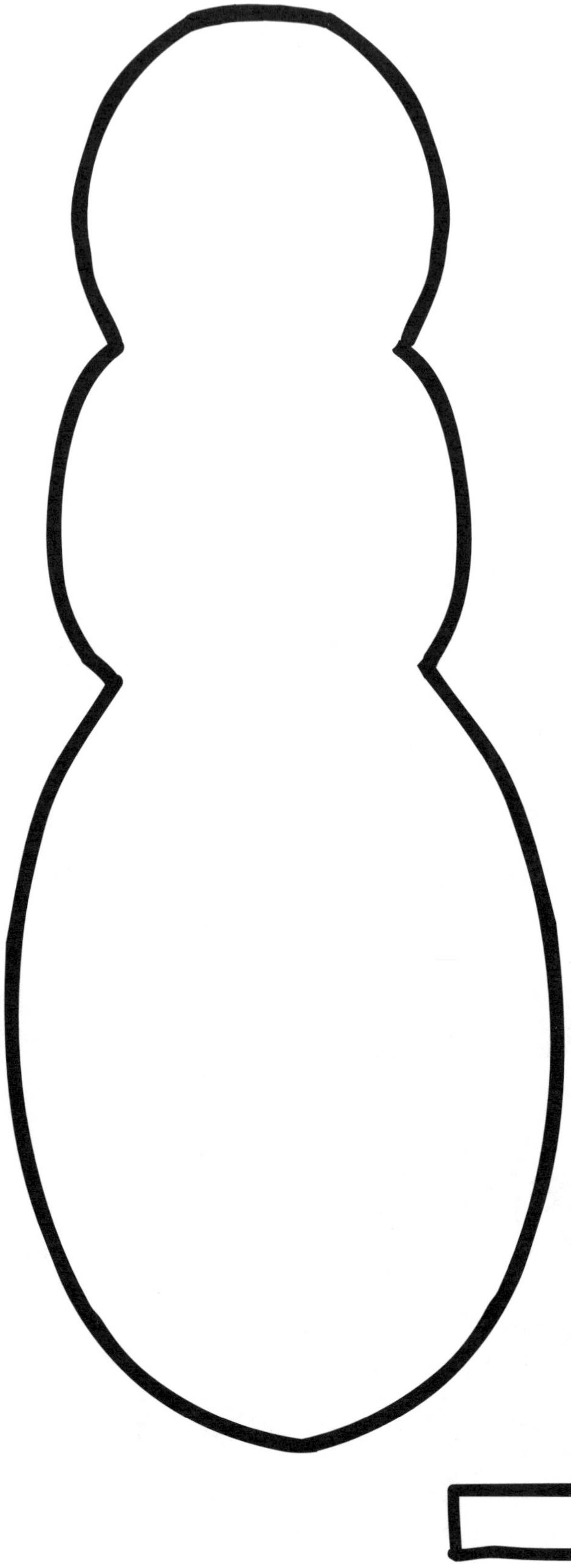

PATTERN A
(Worker Ant Body and Head)

PATTERN C
(Ant Antenna)

PATTERN B
(Ant Leg)

May be duplicated for classroom use.
©1996 by The Regents of the University of California
LHS GEMS—*Ant Homes Under the Ground*

Ant Farm Activity Sheet

May be duplicated for classroom use.
©1996 by The Regents of the University of California
LHS GEMS—*Ant Homes Under the Ground*

Fill the Hill #1

3 scout ants

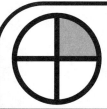

Fill the Hill #1

1 grasshopper and 1 ant

May be duplicated for classroom use.
©1996 by The Regents of the University of California
LHS GEMS—*Ant Homes Under the Ground*

Fill the Hill #1

2 guard ants

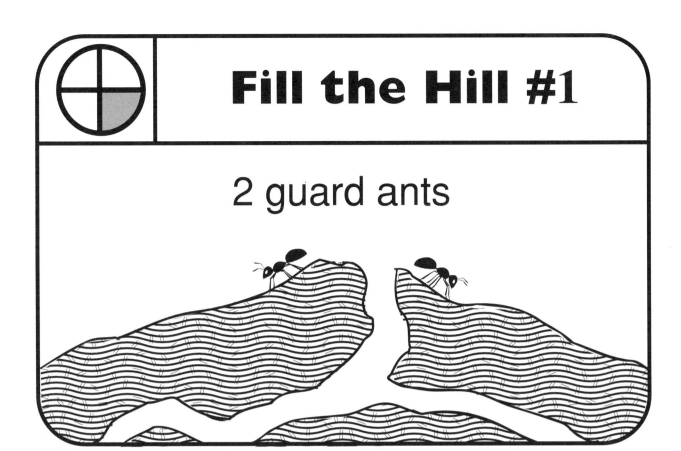

Fill the Hill #1

4 eggs

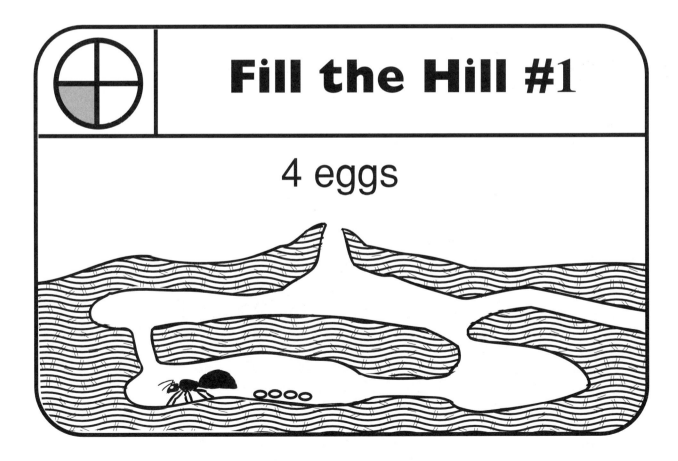

May be duplicated for classroom use.
©1996 by The Regents of the University of California
LHS GEMS—*Ant Homes Under the Ground*

Fill the Hill #2

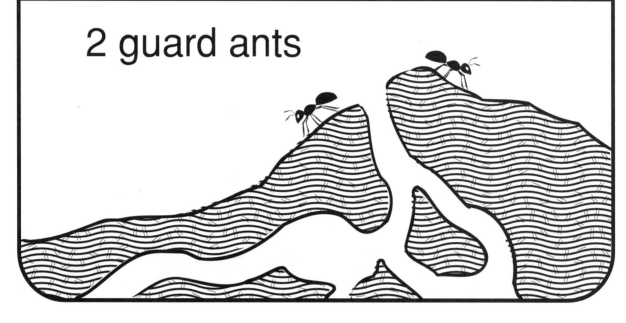

2 guard ants

Fill the Hill #2

5 scout ants

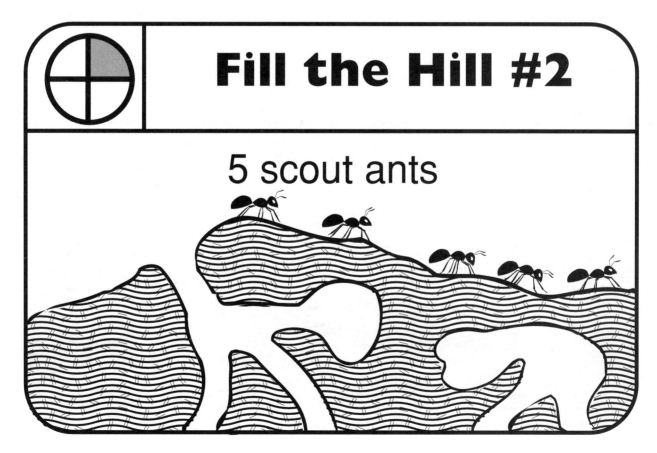

May be duplicated for classroom use.
©1996 by The Regents of the University of California
LHS GEMS—*Ant Homes Under the Ground*

Fill the Hill #2

1 caterpillar and 2 ants

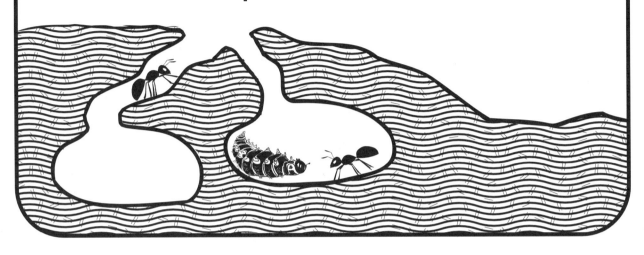

Fill the Hill #2

6 eggs

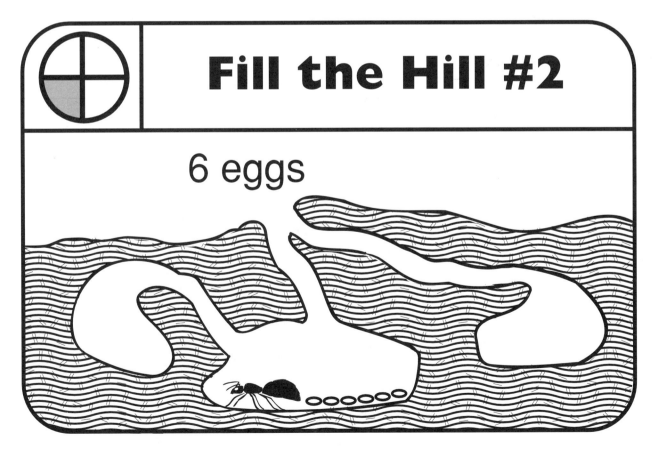

May be duplicated for classroom use.
©1996 by The Regents of the University of California
LHS GEMS—*Ant Homes Under the Ground*

Fill the Hill #3

2 caterpillars and 3 ants

Fill the Hill #3

3 guard ants

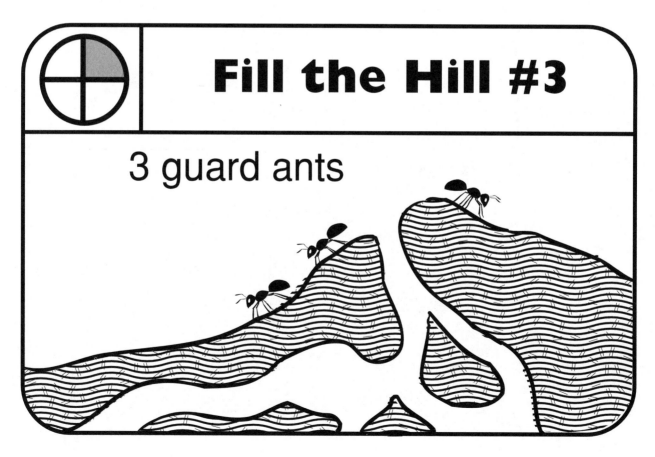

May be duplicated for classroom use.
©1996 by The Regents of the University of California
LHS GEMS—*Ant Homes Under the Ground*

Fill the Hill #3

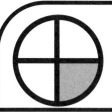

2 grasshoppers

Fill the Hill #3

6 scout ants

May be duplicated for classroom use.
©1996 by The Regents of the University of California
LHS GEMS—*Ant Homes Under the Ground*

Fill the Hill #4

2 housekeeper ants

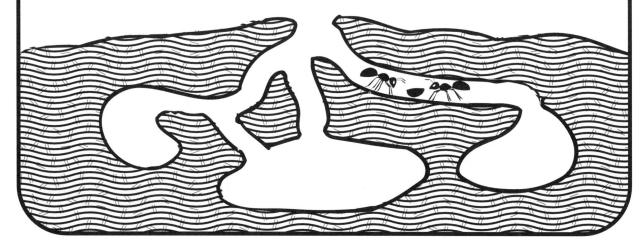

Fill the Hill #4

4 scout ants

May be duplicated for classroom use.
©1996 by The Regents of the University of California
LHS GEMS—*Ant Homes Under the Ground*

Fill the Hill #4

2 grasshoppers

Fill the Hill #4

5 nurse ants and 3 eggs

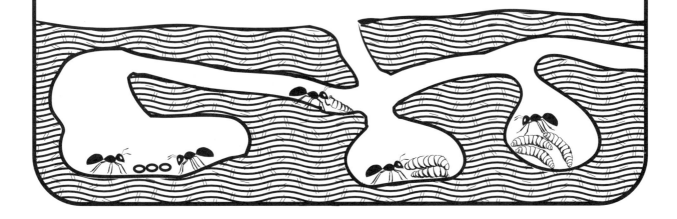

May be duplicated for classroom use.
©1996 by The Regents of the University of California
LHS GEMS—*Ant Homes Under the Ground*

Fill the Hill #5

3 caterpillars and 6 ants

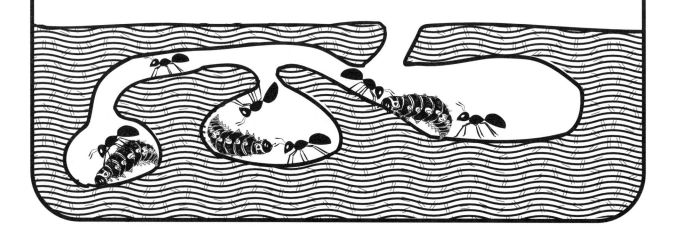

Fill the Hill #5

4 guard ants

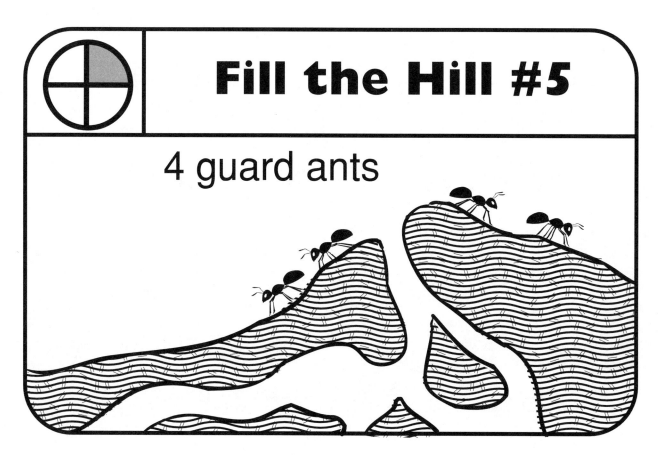

May be duplicated for classroom use.
©1996 by The Regents of the University of California
LHS GEMS—*Ant Homes Under the Ground*

Fill the Hill #5

8 eggs with the queen ant

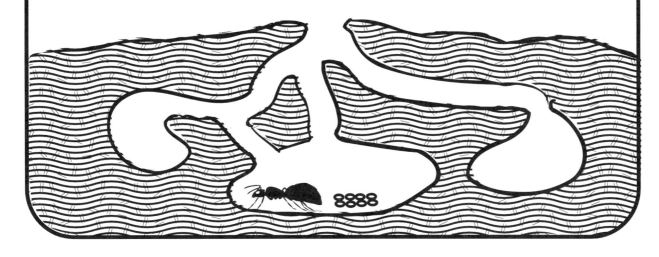

Fill the Hill #5

6 nurse ants

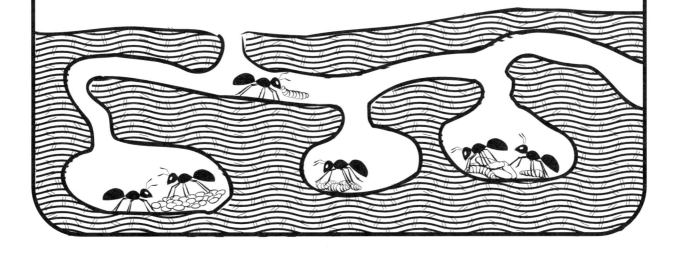

May be duplicated for classroom use.
©1996 by The Regents of the University of California
LHS GEMS—*Ant Homes Under the Ground*

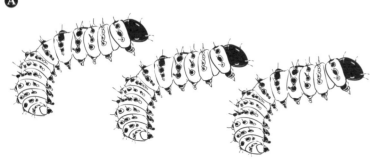

3 caterpillars

3 guard ants

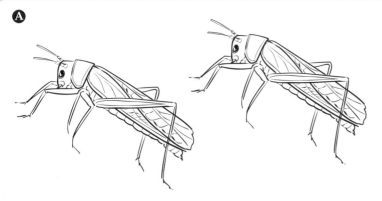

2 grasshoppers

2 scout ants

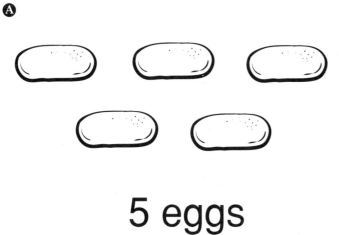

5 eggs

5 nurse ants

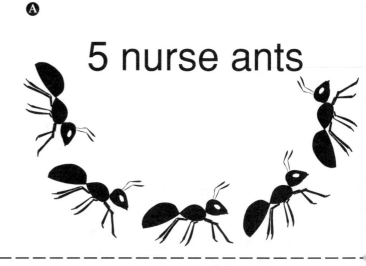

2 crackers

May be duplicated for classroom use.
©1996 by The Regents of the University of California
LHS GEMS—*Ant Homes Under the Ground*

4 housekeeper ants

B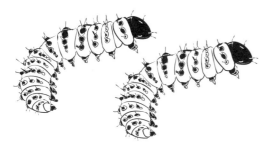

2 caterpillars

B

2 guard ants

B

1 grasshopper

B

4 scout ants

3

3 eggs

B

3 nurse ants

3

1 cracker

B

2 housekeeper ants

May be duplicated for classroom use.
©1996 by The Regents of the University of California
LHS GEMS—*Ant Homes Under the Ground*

The word "themes" is used in many different ways in our daily lives and in educational circles. In the GEMS series, themes are key recurring ideas that cut across all the scientific disciplines. Themes are bigger than facts, concepts, or theories. They link various theories from many disciplines. They also have been described as "the sap that runs through the curriculum," in the sense that they permeate through and arise from the curriculum. By listing the themes that run through a particular GEMS unit on the title page, you can see how the unit fits into the "big picture" of science and connects to other GEMS units. The theme "Patterns of Change," for example, suggests that the unit or some important part of it exemplifies larger scientific ideas about why, how, and in what ways change takes place, whether it is a chemical reaction or a caterpillar becoming a butterfly. GEMS has selected ten major themes:

WHAT ARE THEMES?

Themes are major, recurring ideas that provide a framework for the science curriculum.

Systems and Interactions

Models and Simulations

Stability

Patterns of Change

Evolution

Scale

Structure

Energy

Matter

Diversity and Unity

If you are interested in investigating themes and the thematic approach to teaching and constructing curriculum, write or call for our handbook, *To Build A House: GEMS and the Thematic Approach to Teaching Science.* For more information about all of our GEMS guides and an order brochure, write or call:

University of California, Berkeley
GEMS
Lawrence Hall of Science #5200
Berkeley, CA 94720-5200

(510) 642-7771
fax: (510) 643-0309